Color in Art

Color in Art

A TRIBUTE TO ARTHUR POPE

with

An Introduction to Color

by Howard T. Fisher

Catalogue and Text

by James M. Carpenter

FOGG ART MUSEUM   HARVARD UNIVERSITY

Cover illustration: The Pope Color Solid
The model defines by means of stretched
cords the overall shape of Arthur Pope's
"three-dimensional diagram" of color
relationships. The color solid here appears
within its enclosing cylinder. The color
swatches illustrate the twelve basic hues, at
high intensity and at their respective
darkness levels, somewhat modified by the
photographer's light source.

Library of Congress Catalog Card
Number 74-78-661.
© 1974 by the President and Fellows of
Harvard College.
All rights reserved. Permission to reproduce
any portion must be obtained from the
Fogg Art Museum.
Printed in the United States of America.

This volume was published on the occasion
of the exhibition *Color in Art,* April 24 -
June 16, 1974.

Unless otherwise noted, all works of art
illustrated are in the collection of the Fogg
Art Museum.

Photographs by James Ufford, Fogg Art
Museum, and Wendell Ray, Colby College.

1500 copies of the catalogue were
designed by Malcolm Grear Designers
type set by Dumar Typesetting Inc.
printed by The Meriden Gravure Company
and Princeton Polychrome Press
on Mohawk Superfine
April 1974

Table of Contents

9   Preface

13   An Introduction to Color *by Howard T. Fisher*

35   Color in Art *by James M. Carpenter*

     Supplement: The Pope Color Solid

95   The Form of the Color Solid *by Arthur Pope, with revisions, additional diagrams, and commentary by Howard T. Fisher*

113 Transforming and Scaling the Color Solid *by Howard T. Fisher*

123 Notes

130 Bibliographies: Published Writings of Arthur Pope and Denman W. Ross with Additional Reading

131 Index

Preface

For more than fifty years color theory in relation to art was fundamental in the Fine Arts curriculum at Harvard. With the idea of form as one of the twin essentials in the visual arts, understanding the way color behaves seemed at least half the key to a reasonable approach to learning about painting and, in part, to the ways in which painting conveys meaning. The theories that gave early twentieth-century instructors in color the confidence to teach also gave a generation of European and American artists the assurance that visual communication was possible in a direct and potent fashion by reducing means to color and form alone. Kandinsky and Delaunay had inherited their convictions—their certainty—from the same sophisticated, scientific, and supremely optimistic century of investigation that had so recently produced Seurat.

The same climate of logic also produced Denman Waldo Ross (1853-1935), who lectured on the theory of design at Harvard from 1899 until his death in 1935, and his student and colleague Arthur Pope (1880-   ), who taught in the Fine Arts Department from 1906 until his retirement in 1949 and also served as Director of the Fogg Museum from 1946 to 1948. Both Ross and Pope believed that understanding the orderly way color functions in painting was basic to critical perception. While both men were talented painters, they were especially concerned to impart to students a knowledge of the means of art so that it could enrich the lives of educated men and women. To them, not to know about color was equivalent to illiteracy; moreover, they were convinced that knowledge about color could be taught in as straightforward a way as reading. While the manipulation of color and form to produce great art was reserved for genius, the basic skills were available to anyone with desire and patience, and the joys of comprehension that awaited such an apprenticeship made the basic Fine Arts course at Harvard among the most popular for students, regardless of whether they hoped to be painters, collectors, or simply civilized and educated people.

Color theory in relation to art was a chaotic discipline in 1900. To formulate a rational and coherent framework that would demonstrate how all colors related each to each in all their infinite variety of tones, affected by proximity and quantity, had inspired system after system. The search for such a framework had implications not only for the artist and the person interested in understanding works of art, but also for the manufacturer of paints or other pigments for artists, for industry, and, perhaps above all, for textile dyers. During the century between the color solid visualized by Philip Otto Runge (1810) and that conceived by Wilhelm Ostwald (1916), the arrangement of colors in relation to each other—with their corresponding implications for effective use—varied enormously, especially with regard to concepts concerning intensity.

Arthur Pope developed a system with an extraordinary capacity to comprehend the variety of color behavior. With characteristic modesty, he insists to this day that he had almost nothing to do with it. In the fall of 1973, at the age of 92, he wrote:

> As to the introduction and text, I suppose that I have to be referred to occasionally; but I don't like being credited with ideas that I have simply taken over or inherited from others—as for instance, the distinction of different "modes"—"Venetian mode"—things I adopted from Denman Ross, and which actually go all the way back to C. H. Moore and Ruskin.
>
> I suppose this does not really matter very much. After all, where do our ideas come from anyway? A completely original idea is very rare. What matters is whether it is a good idea or not.
>
> Actually, our whole point of view in teaching—working along side by side with students on the same problem—goes back far beyond Ruskin, to the instruction offered and obtained in Renaissance or medieval workshops.

So, it is appropriate to indicate here the names of those Harvard students who over many years worked side by side with Professor Pope to advance the ideas that are once again presented in this exhibition and its catalogue. Not merely a committee of honor, but a group which has worked with Arthur Pope to develop a set of concepts that will be found to be as useful, as challenging, and as lively as ever! Morton C. Bradley, Richard D. Buck, Anthony M. Clark, Charles C. Cunningham, Sr., Alfred Jakstas, George L. Stout, John Walker, Otto Wittman, and especially James M. Carpenter and Howard T. Fisher, authors of the texts in this publication.

To these, to all of whom the Fogg is grateful, we should also like to add special thanks to Agnes Mongan—who first supported the idea of the exhibition—and to Julianne de Vere, Suzannah Doeringer, Linn Orear, Judith Auerbach; to Susan J. Belton and Margaret Nutting at Colby College; and also to our colleagues at the Boston Museum of Science, who are pursuing a related exhibition, *Color Around Us,* which is likely to be of great interest to the general public.

We join Howard Fisher in expressing our particular appreciation to Arthur Pope, as well as to the persons and organizations mentioned on the following pages. Without their help, his contributions to this publication would not have been possible.

And finally we are grateful to the Munsell Color Foundation for their generous financial assistance towards the color reproductions in this catalogue.

Daniel Robbins
Director

SPECIAL ACKNOWLEDGMENTS

The Fogg Art Museum and Howard T. Fisher are especially grateful to the following:

Richard I. Land, Research Associate in Harvard's Division of Engineering and Applied Physics, provided many helpful suggestions and much valued criticism. Carl E. Foss, color scientist and consultant of Princeton, N.J., kindly commented on manuscript drafts, and gave invaluable advice and assistance regarding the printing of the color charts. J. G. C. Yule, Irving Pobboravsky, and Milton L. Pearson of the Graphic Arts Research Center of the Rochester Institute of Technology kindly spent a day in discussion with Howard Fisher at their laboratory, and subsequently provided much helpful correspondence over almost three years. Mr. Pobboravsky kindly undertook to prepare a special computer program to facilitate conversions between the 4-color printing process and the C.I.E. system.

Arthur C. Hardy, pioneering color scientist and Professor Emeritus of Optics and Photography at the Massachusetts Institute of Technology, patiently answered many questions by letter and in personal meetings. Dorothy Nickerson, Kenneth L. Kelly, and the late Deane B. Judd, distinguished color scientists of the National Bureau of Standards, generously gave advice and information. Fred W. Billmeyer, Jr. and Max Saltzman, of Rensselaer Polytechnic Institute and its Color Measurement Laboratory, were also extremely helpful. Especially appreciated is the technical aid furnished by Mr. Saltzman, as Senior Scientist and Manager of Color Technology with the Allied Chemical Corporation. The help of Gary G. Field and William D. Scheaffer of the Graphic Arts Technical Foundation is also acknowleged. Sanzo Wada, President of the Japan Color Research Institute, provided a copy of its superb *Munsell Renotation Color Book,* arranged in terms of constant-darkness slices.

Laurence W. Engdahl and Ursula Jordan of the Kollmorgen Company arranged for the opportunity to try out their firm's remarkable computer-controlled KCS-40 instrument by scoring numerous research color samples. William N. Hale, Jr. and his associates of Kollmorgen's Munsell Division were also helpful during a day spent at their headquarters in Baltimore. A. R. Brose and C. Ray Bradley of the ByChrome Company patiently provided long replies to long letters relative to the mysteries of the 4-color printing process, and made available their company's excellent material on color printing. The Container Corporation of America gave access to its superb publication on the Ostwald color system, and Pantone, Inc. made available its material on the 4-color printing process. The Direct Image Corporation and Consolidated International Corporation contributed color sample books.

James M. Carpenter produced the color swatches incorporated in the models built and established the initial specifications upon which the color charts are based. Nathaniel J. Jacobson provided advice on artists' pigments and produced a large-scale presentation of colors on the surface of the Pope color solid, to be seen in the related exhibition *Color Around Us* at the Boston Museum of Science.

Isabel P. Conant, Lydia P. Turtle, and Priscilla Pope kindly gave encouragement and financial assistance for research on color relationships and their representation in geometric terms. The Ford Foundation provided closely related assistance.

Maurice D. Kilbridge, Dean of Harvard's Graduate School of Design, cooperated by providing essential work space and secretarial aid, and Allan H. Schmidt, Kathleen M. Reine, and David E. Sheehan, of the Laboratory for Computer Graphics and Spatial Analysis, cooperated in numerous ways.

Without the day-by-day thinking and assistance of the regular staff associates of the Harvard University Mapping Service, little could have been accomplished. Eliza McClennen and Herbert Heidt aided in research, constructed the models of the Pope color solid and related displays, and produced the black and white charts and diagrams presented in this catalogue. Numerous part-time or former staff members also aided, particularly: Hildreth Burnett who did pioneering work on the mapping of color space; Eleanor Hight who refined the methodology finally used; and Carolyn C. Weiss who provided helpful editorial advice and retyping of the manuscript under difficult conditions.

An Introduction to Color

Howard T. Fisher

Color is a psychological phenomenon. It exists exclusively in the mind of the beholder. There is no color as such in nature. Just as there is no sound when a tree falls or lightning strikes in an uninhabited land, so there is no color when the sun rises and flowers open.

The sensation of color is usually caused by variations in the length of light waves radiated by self-luminous sources, reflected from objects, or transmitted through them.[1] The rays enter the eye and through receptors in the eye their nature is communicated by the optic nerve to the brain. Because no two eyes and no two brains may operate in exactly the same way, no two persons are likely to sense color in exactly the same way.[2]

When all visible wavelengths simultaneously enter the eye in suitable force, the sensation called *white* is produced. When only some wavelengths are present, the sensation of *hue* is normally produced, the particular hue depending upon just which wavelengths are present and in what force.

When the wavelengths present are relatively short, the sensation is that of violet. Wavelengths that are still shorter produce what is known as ultraviolet, but these are invisible to the eye. As the wavelengths become longer, the sensations of hue that are produced range progressively through blue, green, yellow, and orange to red. Wavelengths that are still longer produce what is known as infrared, but as with ultraviolet wavelengths these are invisible to the eye.

The fact that white light is composed of a variety of wavelengths can be easily demonstrated by the use of a triangular prism. Rays of light passing obliquely into a clear material such as glass are bent differently depending upon their wavelength. In consequence, if the surfaces of the material are other than parallel, as with a triangular prism, the various wavelengths of light become increasingly separated. When white light is thus broken into its constitutent parts, the mind experiences all the possible color sensations of what is known as the spectrum—that is, all hues between violet and red inclusive.

Raindrops can similarly separate white light into its constituent parts, thus producing a rainbow. It is usual to think of the rainbow as containing every possible hue, but in fact purple, which on the traditional color circle lies between red and violet, is not included. To achieve the sensation known as purple it is necessary to combine light from both ends of the spectrum. Light of short wavelength (violet or near-violet) and light of long wavelength (red or near-red) must simultaneously enter the eye and their combined presence be communicated to the brain.

In the discussion that follows we will be concerned primarily with light as reflected by surfaces. The term *chromatic* will be used to designate colors possessing hue, and the terms *neutral* or *achromatic* will designate all possible gra-

The following charts illustrate the nature of color differences in terms of the Pope color solid. The first chart is of an introductory nature, with emphasis on hues of high intensity and the various darkness levels (2-8) which are associated with them.

The remaining three charts show in each case the same set of 166 colors so organized as to emphasize slices through the solid which are constant in hue (color chart 2), constant in darkness (color chart 3), and constant in intensity (color chart 4). For more detailed explanation see the Supplement.

Neutrals, shown in color chart 1, have been omitted from the other three charts in order to permit the chromatic color samples to be larger than would otherwise be possible. For the same reason the constant-darkness slices in color chart 3 have been separated at yellow and opened out (as suggested in their accompanying small diagrams).

These charts have been produced mechanically by offset lithography through the use of the standard 4-color process.* As in all printing work, the colors achieved are not perfect, but they may serve to suggest the nature of the variability present within color space.

*The standard 4-color process is based on the use of dots of varying size, printed in yellow, magenta, cyan, and black. In theory, if the inks could be perfect, the black would not be needed. In a very real sense, the process uses five colors in that white, provided by the paper, is also essential. In order to be below the resolving power of the eye, it is usual to employ 133 dots to the linear inch or 17,689 per square inch—for a total of 70,756 when all four inks are used.

For reproducing illustrations of art objects, photography is used, a separate plate being made for each color through the use of a filter. For the production of graphic work, such as the color charts in this book, the plates can be made by mechanical rather than photographic means, through the specification of the dot sizes required. The usual percentages (other than 0 for no ink, and 100 for solid ink) are 5, 10, 20, 30, 40, 50, 60, 70, 80, and 90. It is best to superimpose inks no more than necessary and most colors can be satisfactorily achieved with not more than two chromatic colors, with or without black. Those interested in exploring the potentialities of 4-color printing by mechanical means should see *By-Chroma 4 Color Charts* (undated), printed and distributed by ByChrome Company, Inc., Box 1077, Columbus, Ohio. This is available in two volumes, one for matte or uncoated paper and one for glossy or coated paper—the latter yielding greater intensities. Each volume contains 19,008 samples. A somewhat similar publication (but omitting combinations based on 5% or, for black, of more than 50%) is available from Pantone, Inc., New York, N.Y. See Deane B. Judd and Günter Wyszecki, *Color in Business, Science, and Industry,* 2nd ed., (New York: John Wiley & Sons, 1963), pp. 214-219; and J. A. C. Yule, *Principles of Color Reproduction* . . . (New York: John Wiley & Sons, 1967). See also note 16 for reference to recent work by Carl E. Foss.

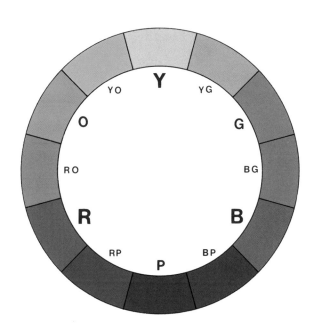

Top: *The traditional color circle, with all samples of high intensity.*

Upper middle: *The color circle cut at yellow and straightened horizontally (yellow repeated left and right).*

Lower middle: *The same, but with samples placed with height conforming to their darkness levels (neutrals shown at right).*

Bottom: *Corresponding samples, but all adjusted to middle darkness or level 5—with only red-orange and blue-green remaining at high intensity.*

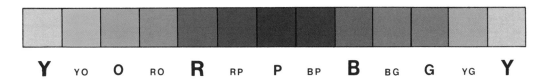

Y YO **O** RO **R** RP **P** BP **B** BG **G** YG **Y**

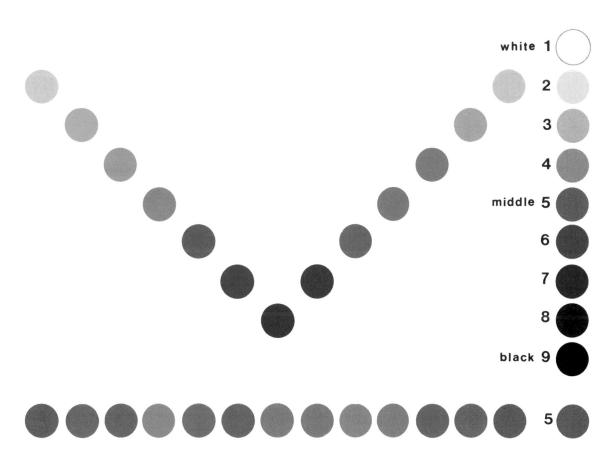

white **1**

2

3

4

middle **5**

6

7

8

black **9**

5

dations of gray, including white and black as the extremes of gray. In the study of color, it is usually convenient to think of neutrals as colors, and they will be so considered here.

It may be useful to start by imagining colors as if they are seen one at a time under white light. Though color is seldom if ever seen in this way, it is helpful to postpone consideration of the fact that whenever two or more colors are seen together they interact upon one another. Accordingly let us imagine that we are looking at a surface (1) sufficiently large to fill our entire field of vision, (2) uniform in character, and (3) evenly illuminated as seen by the viewer.[3]

If the assumed surface reflects equally light of all wavelengths, it will be neutral—that is, it will be achromatic. If the surface reflects light of some wavelengths more than others, it will be chromatic, that is, it will be characterized by hue—the exact hue depending upon the particular wavelengths reaching the eye, as well as upon the strength of the wavelengths. There can be exceptions to this statement under certain circumstances. When the wavelengths are balanced in relation to neutral, the result will be neutral.[4] Hue results from an imbalance among the wavelengths of light. In other words, when some wavelengths are weak or absent hue will result if among the wavelengths reflected there is an imbalance in relation to neutral.

If the surface is of neutral color, capable of reflecting equally and strongly light of all visible wavelengths, it will still never be capable of reflecting all of the light that falls upon it. No matter how nonabsorbent of light the surface may be, some of the light falling upon it will necessarily be absorbed by it. (Ordinary white paper, for example, absorbs about 16% of the light falling upon it.) If the amount absorbed is relatively small (and the amount reflected thus relatively large), the surface will be white or near-white. If the amount absorbed is more substantial, the surface will be gray—the greater the amount absorbed, the darker the gray. If the amount absorbed is relatively large (and the amount reflected thus relatively small), the surface will be black or near-black. No matter how absorbent of light the surface may be, some of the light falling upon it will necessarily be reflected by it.

To try to judge colors under isolated circumstances, however, is extremely difficult. When one color only is to be seen, there is nothing to serve as a basis for comparison and judgment. Not even the viewer's imperfect memory of past colors experienced is likely to prove of much help. In consequence, even the most intense effort to estimate the degree of lightness or darkness present may prove highly inaccurate. There would be considerable difficulty in trying to decide, for example, whether the gray color observed was light, medium, or dark. Similarly, assuming that the strength of the viewing light were only roughly known (which would be the case in real life situations), it would be impossible to differentiate between the darkness of a relatively light surface in a weak light and the darkness of a relatively dark surface in a strong light.

Even if another neutral of a somewhat different darkness were to be included within the field of vision, it would still be difficult to judge the degree of darkness present in the original color. We could say that it was lighter or darker than the second color but not much else. In order to judge with any confidence the darkness of an achromatic color, examples of both white or near-white and black or near-black would also have to be present. Otherwise, nothing can serve as a basis for comparison and judgment. Some musicians may have absolute pitch, but nothing comparable exists in relation to color. To judge darkness among chromatic colors presents problems of a similar but more difficult nature.

As we have seen, whenever the wavelengths and strength of the light reflected by a surface are out of balance in relation to neutral, hue will be present. If the imbalance is small, the color will be chromatic to at least some slight extent. If the wavelengths reflected are out of balance to a greater degree, what we will call the *intensity* of the resulting color will be greater. As the imbalance among the wavelengths increases, intensity increases as well, until all sense of grayness is lost. As with darkness, if but a single color is seen with nothing to serve as a basis for comparison, our judgment of the degree of intensity will be extremely rough at best. It would be difficult if not impossible, for example, to decide whether a certain color was of low as compared with medium intensity.

Even if a neutral (of the same darkness) were to be included within the field of vision, it would still be difficult to judge the degree of intensity present in the original color. We could say that it was more or less intense than the second color but not much else. In order to be able to judge with any confidence the intensity of a chromatic color, examples of both neutral and high intensity for the same hue at the same darkness should also be present. Thus color, even more than the weather, is from man's viewpoint inherently relative in nature. It is normally judged in terms of the overall context of our surroundings. In the absence of "benchmarks" to serve as a basis for comparison, it can be all but impossible to make judgments about color.

In the examples just given, differentiations were made in terms of the color qualities of darkness or intensity, but similar difficulties arise in terms of hue differentiation. If seen in total isolation it may be impossible to judge hues except very roughly. Even if some other hues are present, it may still be difficult to judge other than roughly. Red-orange, for example, in the absence of the adjacent hues red and orange might be judged simply as red, though no nearer to red than to orange—especially since red seems to be a more basic hue in terms of human experience. Yet for the purposes of this discussion it will frequently be helpful to think about colors as if seen individually.

COLOR CHART 2 *Constant-Hue Slices*

Color at standard sampling locations for the Pope color solid, with neutrals omitted to save space.

Upper left: Yellow, the lightest hue, with warm colors following across the top.

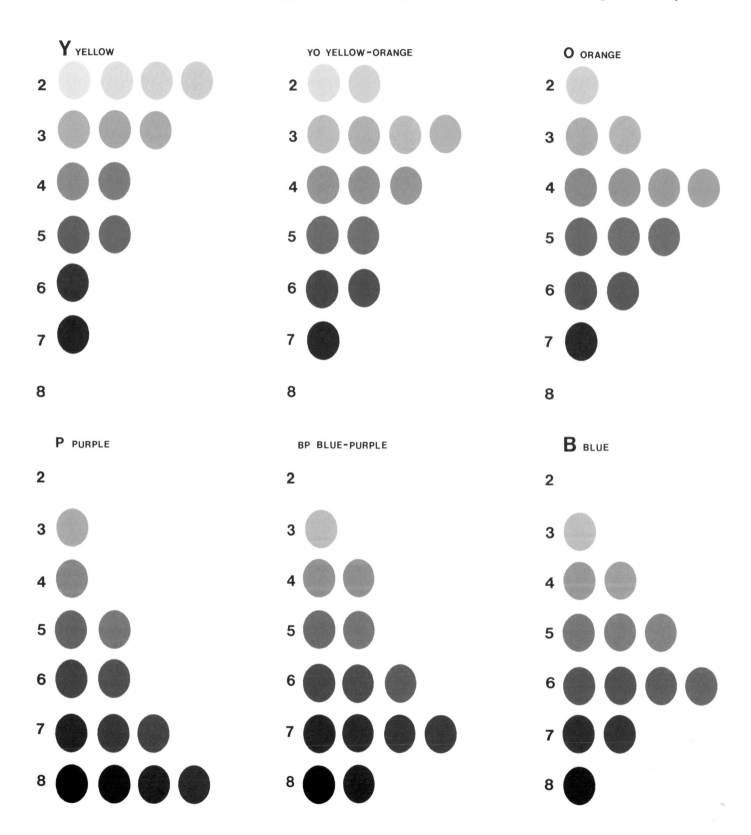

Lower left: *Purple, the darkest hue, with cool colors following across the bottom.*

Among the samples for each slice (or constant-hue triangle), intensities increase from left to right, starting with 25% and going through 50% and 75% to 100% (at the extreme right).

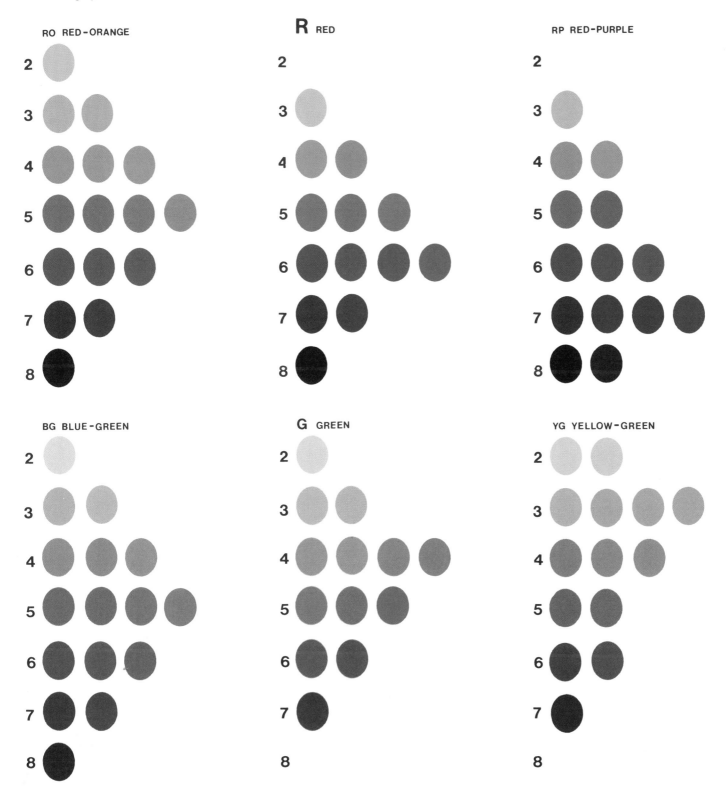

RO RED-ORANGE

R RED

RP RED-PURPLE

BG BLUE-GREEN

G GREEN

YG YELLOW-GREEN

When hue results from the unbalanced absorption of wavelengths by an opaque object, it is the result of a *subtractive* process; that is, hue is the consequence of the removal or subtraction of light of certain wavelengths. Once absorbed they are not reflected and any resulting imbalance creates the sensation of hue. For example, if blue wavelengths are absorbed, the remaining wavelengths will give the sensation of yellow. If red wavelengths are absorbed, the remaining wavelengths will give the sensation of blue-green (sometimes called cyan).

The subtractive process is at work whenever a material selectively absorbs certain wavelengths, while reflecting others. This is also the case when light passes through a light-permeable material that absorbs or scatters certain wavelengths, such as colored plastic, or glass, or perhaps a colored varnish or glaze.

In contrast, there is an *additive* process. If we start with light sources of two or more colors rather than with white or balanced light, they can be combined to produce other colors. For example, if we combine light having the wavelengths of red and green, the result will be the sensation of yellow. If we combine light having the wavelengths of red and blue, the result will be the sensation of red-purple, usually called magenta. If we combine the wavelengths of red, green, and blue in suitable strengths we will get neutral, since those hues are capable of being balanced in relation to neutral. The additive process is also involved when light of different colors is reflected to the eye from two or more closely spaced surfaces. This can be achieved by placing different colors on a rotating disk, or by intermixing small dots of color as in color television or in Pointillist painting.

While the distinctive concepts of the subtractive and additive processes are important to understand from a theoretical viewpoint, it should be recognized that in practice the two usually operate in combination, as for example if a colored glaze is used over a Pointillist painting. The subtractive process would be involved in the case of the pigments, the additive process in the case of the small dots of color, and the subtractive process again in the case of the glaze.

To distinguish clearly between the two processes can at times be extremely difficult. The standard 4-color printing process, by which the color plates in this publication are produced, provides an excellent illustration of this. White paper is overprinted in widely varying combination with small dots of black, cyan, magenta, and yellow—with the last three inks being transparent to some degree. The results represent such an intimate mixture of additive and subtractive processes that only a qualified color scientist would be able to provide an adequate explanation of exactly what has taken place.

When a person looks at an opaque object, the light finally entering the eye may have come originally from any of several different types of sources or combinations of sources. Furthermore, in traveling to the eye it may have been altered in any of several possible ways or combinations of ways. The original source is always some self-luminous "object"—such as the sun, a gas flame, an electric arc, or the filament of a light bulb. The light from such sources would not necessarily be white, and if lacking or weak in any of the wavelengths found in white light it might influence to at least some extent the final colors seen. As an extreme example, if a painting or other art object were viewed under a green light no colors other than green or neutral would be visible. It is of the greatest importance to recognize that whenever paintings are seen under light that is not white or near-white, their appearance may be significantly affected.

In traveling from the original source to the object being observed, the light may pass (in whole or in part) through some material, such as colored plastic or glass, that is capable of altering its characteristics by absorbing or scattering some of the original wavelengths.

The light that finally reaches the object will in part be reflected back to the eye. Such reflection will seldom come exclusively from the extreme outer surface of the object.[5] The rays of light will usually enter the object to at least some extent and be internally deflected, perhaps several times, by particles within it. Finally, they will be partially absorbed by the object and partially reflected back to the eye. The material of the observed object may thus serve as a filter as well as a reflector of the light rays.[6]

An infinite variety of possibilities exists for the original source or sources of the viewing light and for the modifying mechanisms to which that light may be subjected before reaching the eye. For the purposes of effectively examining opaque works of art, we must assume that the viewing light is white or near-white, thus containing all or essentially all the wavelengths present in visible light. Given this assumption, all that need concern us is the portion of the original visible wavelengths that finally reaches the eye. Only rarely will there be any reason to explore the particular processes involved: whether the modification of the original light is determined exclusively by a subtractive or an additive process or, as will usually be the case, by some combination of the two. In the discussion that follows we will be dealing with *surface color*—color caused by the reflection of light from a surface, with the surface made visible by white light of adequate brightness to permit it to be clearly seen.[7]

To summarize thus far in the simplest possible terms: white light contains all colors, although they cannot be seen individually. They become separate and visible, however, if the different colors are dispersed, as by a triangular prism.[8] When white light shines upon an opaque object some wavelengths may be absorbed and thus no longer seen. Others are reflected, and these serve to give the object its color.

COLOR CHART 3   *Constant-Darkness Slices*

Color at standard sampling locations for the Pope color solid, with neutrals omitted to save space.

Yellow in each case is repeated left and right, with purple in the center; warm colors appear on the left and cool colors on the right. Among the samples for each slice, intensities increase from the top downward, starting with 25% and going through 50% and 75% to 100% (at the bottom).

The small diagrams show how the color circle has in each case been cut at yellow and opened out to permit the display of samples of adequate size.

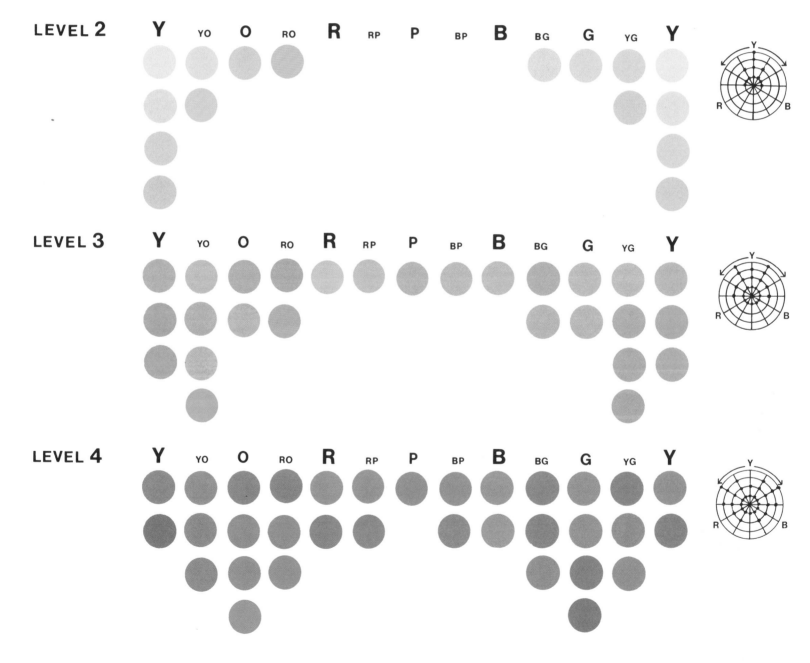

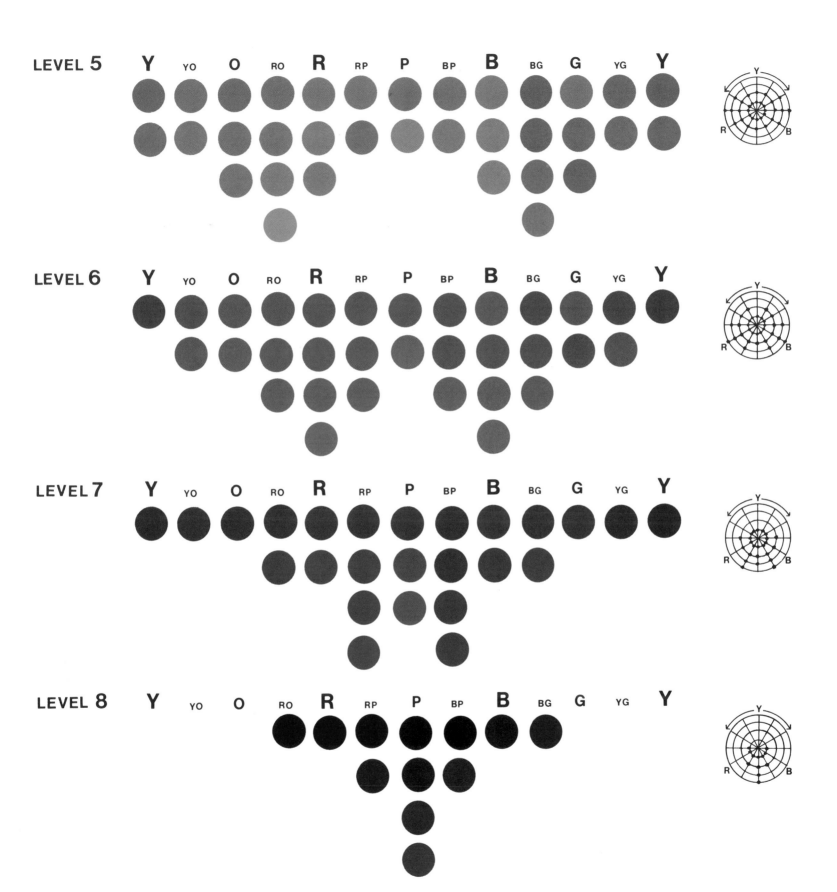

LEVEL 5   Y   YO   O   RO   R   RP   P   BP   B   BG   G   YG   Y

LEVEL 6   Y   YO   O   RO   R   RP   P   BP   B   BG   G   YG   Y

LEVEL 7   Y   YO   O   RO   R   RP   P   BP   B   BG   G   YG   Y

LEVEL 8   Y   YO   O   RO   R   RP   P   BP   B   BG   G   YG   Y

23

When we see color, its three "dimensions"—*lightness and darkness, hue,* and *intensity*—are sensed simultaneously. But when we think about color, each must be given separate consideration. For a meaningful description of color in terms of art each dimension must be defined at least roughly. A clear understanding of each, with emphasis on appearance rather than process, will be important.

Darkness or "Value"

The dimension of *lightness and darkness* varies continuously between the two end points of white and black. For simplicity, since our concern here will be primarily with paintings and designs (typically produced on a white or near-white background), we will use the term *darkness* or the alternative word "value" which is frequently used in art education and criticism.[9]

Darkness (or "value") applies to every example of surface color, whether achromatic (devoid of hue, or neutral) or chromatic (possessing hue). In broad terms, the concept is easily comprehensible, but unfortunately no general agreement exists about how white and black should be defined or how the darkness range should be subdivided.

The usual approach to the problem is to try to divide the range of grays between white and black (regardless of just how those words may be defined) into visually equal steps. In attempting to do this, however, numerous difficulties are encountered. Study has been devoted to the problem for more than a hundred years, and a wide variety of solutions has been proposed.

The difficulty arises because apparent darkness is not proportional to the light reflected by neutral surfaces, and the particular viewing circumstances strongly influence what is seen by the viewer. For example, when gray areas are examined individually their appearance will be strongly influenced by the nature of the background against which they are seen. Thus a darkness scale in terms of visually equal spacing can only be for a particular background darkness. A person's ability to distinguish among grays is greatest when the grays are similar in darkness to their background. Thus, against a light background differences among light grays will be more easily distinguished, while against a dark background differences among dark grays will be more easily distinguished. The size of the samples used and the width of any spaces left between them also influence their appearance, and hence what constitutes visually equal spacing. In brief, no single darkness scale can be considered appropriate under all circumstances, even for neutrals.

If the samples or background, or both, are chromatic, the difficulties are far more complicated. Different hues are characterized by different darkness progressions, and higher intensity in and of itself makes hues appear less dark.

The problem is further complicated by the fact that colors in art are seldom, if ever, neatly arranged in order of increasing darkness against a uniform background. Each color, even if sometimes thought of individually, tends to be seen against other colors, and in most instances any color will appear against a variety of backgrounds. We thus have what is known as a "complex field"—and research into visually equal darkness scales in terms of complex fields is still very much in its infancy.

Exactly what scale of darkness should be employed is thus far from clear. For the purposes here, however, the concept of various levels of darkness is sufficiently well understood and need not be more precisely defined.*

Hue

The dimension of hue varies continuously and may be plotted in a circle, as with compass direction or clock time. (See color chart 1.) Since there are no end points on a circle, in order to think and talk about hue one or more reference locations must be arbitrarily set. Here again, as with darkness, there is no general agreement on how many there should be, where they should be placed, what they should represent, or what they should be called. The most common approach—and an especially useful one to artists, designers, and art critics—is what we may refer to as the 12-hue circuit. It is derived from the convenient concept of red, yellow, and blue as primary colors, with spacing identical to that of the hour positions on the face of a clock.[10] Yellow, as the lightest of all the hues, appears at the top of the color circle at the position of 12 o'clock.[11] Blue may then be placed at 4 o'clock and red at 8 o'clock, with the other nine hues at appropriate intervening locations.

In diagramming color relationships it is frequently convenient to cut the color circle at some point and stretch it out in a straight horizontal line. (See color chart 1.) For our purposes the cut may best be made at yellow, in which event the basic twelve hues would appear as in the sequence at the left.

Thus, in English, the colors of the 12-hue circuit can all be expressed through the use of six common words. While numerous other hue designations exist, every possible hue may be defined in terms of these six words. For example, the word *magenta* may be defined as a red-purple, the word *cyan* as a blue-green, or the word *pink* as a light red. But what shade of red, orange, yellow, green, blue, or purple these six words convey is not clear. One person's red may be another's red-orange, or one person's blue may be another's blue-green. For the

Suggested Terms and Abbreviations

yellow	Y	
yellow-orange	YO	
orange	O	*Referred to here as "warm" hues*
red-orange	RO	
red	R	
red-purple	RP	
purple	P	
blue-purple	BP	
blue	B	
blue-green	BG	*Referred to here as "cool" hues*
green	G	
yellow-green	YG	
yellow (repeated)	Y	

*For a discussion of the problem of darkness scaling, see the Supplement, pp. 115-117.

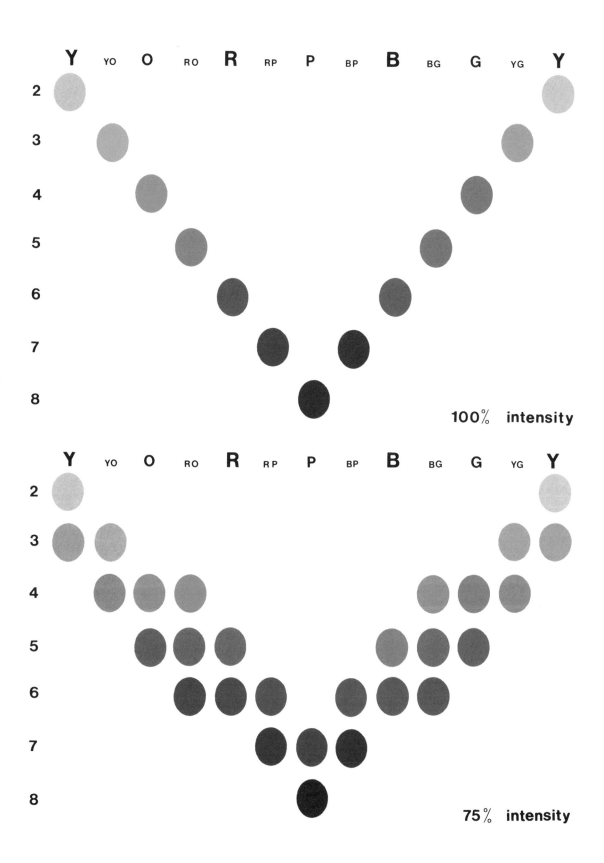

100% intensity

75% intensity

Yellow in each case is repeated left and right, with purple in the center; warm colors appear on the left and cool colors on the right. Among the samples for each slice, darkness increases from the top downward.

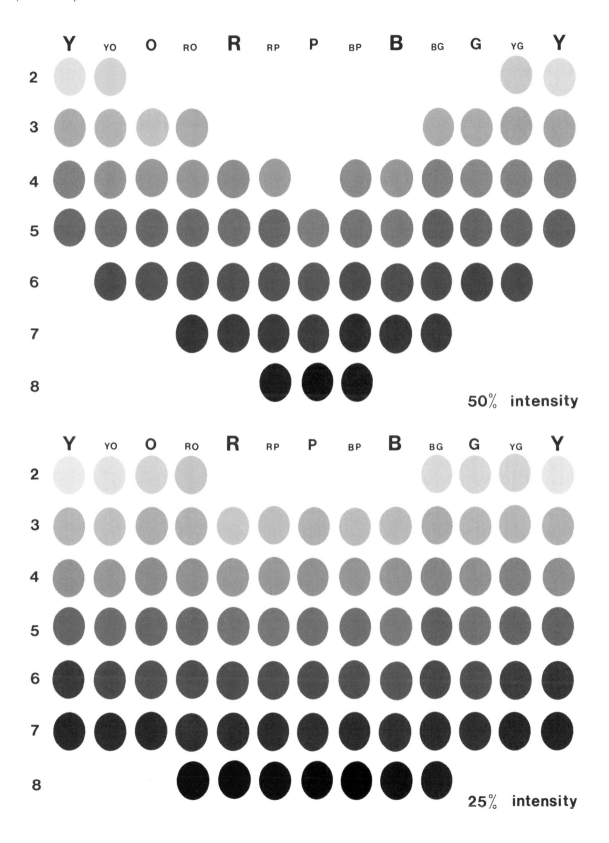

purposes here, however, the terms are sufficiently well understood and need not be more precisely defined.

The variable of hue applies only to chromatic surface colors. Neutrals or achromatic colors are totally devoid of hue. Unfortunately there is no general agreement as to just how the color circle should be subdivided for *scaling* purposes; that is, just what hues should be selected to correspond to the hue names.*

Intensity

The third dimension, *intensity*, varies continuously with an increasing magnitude that starts at neutral and proceeds to some maximum. In relation to art it is best measured in relative terms for each hue separately, between the two assumed end points of 0% for neutral and 100% for high intensity.

A color of low relative intensity will be close to the gray of neutral—only slightly differentiated from gray. A color of high relative intensity will be far from gray giving an impression of purity, in the sense of freedom from all grayness. This quality of intensity is sometimes expressed in other terms, as in the Munsell color notation system. For the artist, designer, or art critic, however, the concept of relative intensity is likely to be far more meaningful. In terms of human experience, we tend to associate the names of hues with the highest intensity commonly encountered with each hue—and then to judge lesser intensities for the same hue relative to the highest intensity. For example, the highest intensity commonly encountered for orange tends to be thought of as inherently characteristic of orange. Similarly, the highest intensity commonly encountered with blue-green tends to be considered inherently characteristic of blue-green. In trying to visualize orange, most people will imagine a high-intensity orange rather than a low-intensity orange, which would have a relatively grayish or brownish cast.

In illustrating the color circle, the concept of relative intensity seems to have been traditionally and generally employed. That is, hues of characteristic high intensity have been used insofar as possible, and all have been placed at a uniform distance from the center of the color circle. Like the variable of hue, the concept of intensity applies only to chromatic surface colors. Neutral or achromatic colors are defined as having an intensity of zero, in either relative or absolute terms.†

Other variables of appearance, such as luster and iridescence, also exist in connection with color, but they will not be considered here. The three variables of darkness, hue, and intensity are, for our purposes, of paramount significance.

*For a discussion of the problem of hue scaling, see the Supplement, pp. 117-118.
†For a discussion of the problem of intensity scaling, see the Supplement, pp. 118-120.

We have tended here to treat colors one at a time; in real life colors are seen in combination. It is hard to imagine any exceptions: perhaps a cloudless sky when looking straight up while lying on the top of a hill, or the inside of a cave in total darkness. Even if we imagine a painting all of one color it will still be seen against a background. It must be recognized that whenever two or more colors are seen together they will without exception interact to some extent. Interaction may be minor and hard to define, but it will usually be an important factor, and may at times have extremely significant and perhaps even startling consequences.[12]

Sensory interaction, of course, is not limited to the sensations of color. To quote a distinguished psychologist: "A gray surface looks red if we have been looking at a blue-green one; plain paper feels smooth if we have been feeling sandpaper or rough if we have been feeling plate glass; and tap water tastes sweet if we have been eating artichokes."[13]

In the case of color, this phenomenon is experienced even with neutrals. A gray tone of medium darkness, for example, will appear light when seen against a dark background—and dark when seen against a light background. In consequence, if a reasonably sized area of uniform darkness is bounded by both lighter and darker tones it will no longer appear to be of uniform darkness.

When different colors are placed in close proximity the *inevitability* of more or less complex interaction *must be anticipated*. For example, if orange is placed adjacent to red it will appear more yellow than if seen alone; if placed next to yellow, it will appear more red than if seen alone. When using color the skilled artist or designer, consciously or unconsciously, will always be aware of this phenomenon, the problems it raises, and the opportunities it affords. Here the painter has a great advantage over some other artists in that he can see what he is creating as he personally executes it. In contrast, the ceramacist or the architect, for example, can seldom have such feedback.

Two kinds of color interaction are usually recognized: *simultaneous contrast* is experienced when colors are seen at the same time in different locations, while *successive contrast* is experienced when colors are seen in succession in either the same or different locations. Since the eye tends to move about when examining the complex fields characteristic of art, the two types of contrast tend to be thoroughly intermixed. The subject of color interaction is far too large and complex to permit more extended treatment here. Those interested in exploring its fascinating ramifications might well start with the writings of Josef Albers, especially his *Interaction of Color*.

A common experience of a closely related nature is frequently referred to by the term *color constancy*. A white tablecloth in shadow or in a dark corner, for example, is accepted and judged as white, although actually seen as gray. Similarly, on a bright sunny day, although winter shadows on snow tend to be seen as blue, the snow is still accepted and judged as white. This phenomenon results from the fact that, in those special cases when the nature of the illumination is clearly apparent, the mind takes it into account and judges the object seen as if illuminated by it. In a painting the illumination may appear to come from a candle or other special source, shown or not shown in the picture, or it may be light reflected in whole or in part from some other object. The wall of a white house would continue to be judged white even if actually rather green as a result of its partial illumination by light reflected from nearby vegetation.

For this phenomenon to operate, however, the logic of the situation must be apparent. If the tablecloth is seen to be gray in the clear presence of a strong white light, it would obviously be accepted as being gray in fact. If the house wall were green in the clear absence of any surrounding foliage or other possible source of green light, it would obviously be accepted as being green in fact.[14]

DISPLAYING COLOR DIMENSIONS IN GEOMETRIC FORM

Geometric representations have customarily been used as a way of making color relationships visually accessible. Everyone is familiar with charts for the graphic representation of any two interrelated variables, such as temperature and time of the year, or income and taxes. When three variables are involved— as with darkness, hue, and intensity—the problem of graphic display tends to become considerably more complex. A three-dimensional "construction" is usually required, with one dimension for each of the variables to be portrayed. This may take the form of a physical model, with three actual dimensions in space; or it may consist of a drawing, representative of such a model; or, for those familiar with the subject matter being portrayed, it may consist of a mental image.

In view of the particular circumstances involved when illustrating color relationships, a physical model can be especially useful for the representation of color space. Models, however, in spite of their inherent virtues for the representation of anything three-dimensional—in either a physical or abstract sense—take considerable amounts of time to construct and are impossible to enclose between the covers of a book. Hence drawings are more usually employed to represent three-dimensional constructions. By their use we may achieve a clearer understanding of color relationships than would otherwise be possible. The ultimate goal, of course, is an easily visualized mental image of color space.

Purposes vary, however, and in the absence of objective scales for appearance factors, there can be no single best solution. Of the many systems devised over the past two hundred years, the most useful for the artist, designer, and art critic is almost certainly that proposed in the early years of this century by Arthur Pope.

The Pope Color Solid

Arthur Pope succeeded in assembling a remarkably revealing color order system that is especially valuable for what scientists would refer to as a *first-order description* of color variability.[15] In this respect the Pope color solid differs markedly from color solids designed to serve other objectives—for example, to illustrate pigment mixtures or printing methods; to serve the needs of scientific quantification; or to provide color scores in psychological terms.[16]

The Pope color solid uses the "dimensions" already presented. It is of double-cone type, based on the use of cylindrical coordinates relative to a central axis representing neutral. The darkness dimension (at nine darknesses) runs vertically, with normally encountered white at the top point and normally encountered black at the bottom point; the hue dimension (at twelve hues) runs circumferentially around the central neutral axis; and the intensity dimension (at five intensities) runs radially out from the neutral axis.

Since systems based on cylindrical coordinates are, however, difficult to represent in drawings, it is frequently convenient to cut the color solid at yellow and stretch it out straight, as with the color circle. (See color chart 1.) This permits all three color variables to be displayed simultaneously. When so transformed, the darkness dimension still runs vertically. The hue dimension, however, runs horizontally (with yellow repeated left and right), while the intensity dimension runs obliquely—so it appears to extend up and out from the "base plane" which represents neutral (or 0% intensity).

Such a transformation may be referred to as a color score. For any chromatic color, darkness is indicated by its position up and down in the drawing, hue is indicated by its position across the width of the drawing, and intensity is indicated by its oblique height or projection.

Pope first proposed his solution around 1910. In its development he was strongly influenced by the work of Denman W. Ross (1853-1935) with whom Pope worked closely at Harvard as both a student and colleague.

Ross began studies at Harvard as a student of economics and history, and he received his Ph.D. there in 1880. He gradually abandoned these subjects, however, to turn his attention to research into the practice and history of painting. He became deeply absorbed with theoretical problems of color in art, and held an appointment at Harvard as Lecturer on the Theory of Design from

1899 until the end of his life. His large classes, based in the School of Architecture and conducted during the summer, were attended by numerous teachers of art drawn from a wide area. In 1907 he published his *Theory of Pure Design*, in which he proposed various color scales and hue triangles of varying shape to show characteristic darkness relationships and illustrate approximate contrasts in darkness and intensity.

Pope, with due credit, made use of the Ross color scales and color triangles in creating his own more advanced concepts, and in 1922 published his *Tone Relations in Painting* in which he expanded the twelve constant-hue triangles of Ross into his three-dimensional color solid. Pope's solid, and diagrams derived from it, appeared again in his revised work, *The Painter's Terms* (1929), and its companion volume, *The Painter's Modes of Expression* (1931). These were later again revised and published as one volume in *The Language of Drawing and Painting* (1949).

Ironically, Ross failed to appreciate the merits of a three-dimensional approach and actually disapproved of Pope's use of his ideas in the concept of a color solid.[17] In a similar way, Pope frequently referred to the lack of accuracy in his own work, not realizing its rather remarkable level of accuracy if judged as a first-order description of the world of color appearance, which was his real objective. In fact, Pope himself failed to appreciate the great value and full significance of the concept of *relative* intensity, upon which all of his work and that of Ross was based.[18]

The years that were so productive for Ross and Pope were years of great ferment in the world of color research, and for a brief period Boston found itself at the center of this activity. At the very time Pope was studying with Denman Ross in Cambridge, Albert H. Munsell (1858-1918) was working on his color sphere. Based on a concept that had been proposed early in the nineteenth century by the German romantic painter Philip Otto Runge (1777-1810), this served as the foundation for what was ultimately developed into the world-famous Munsell color notation system. It may also be noted that in 1905 Wilhelm Ostwald (1853-1932), renowned physical chemist from Leipzig (and later winner of the Nobel Prize in chemistry), came to give a series of lectures at the Massachusetts Institute of Technology. While in Boston he met Munsell and, stimulated by what he saw of his work, he shortly thereafter initiated his own distinguished career in the field of color study.[19]

As with all color appearance systems, those of Pope and Munsell were based on the use of subjective scales, in contrast to the objective scales used by physicists with color measuring instruments. The Munsell system has now been standardized in relation to what is known as the C.I.E. system used by color scientists, and hence is well suited to the purposes of psychological scoring and the production of standardized sample swatches. The Pope color solid, however, offers a number of advantages from the viewpoint of general comprehension as well as for the purposes of the artist, designer, and art critic. It is simple and smooth in shape, symmetrical about three planes, and possesses the great merit of a fixed exterior form. This is in marked contrast to the Munsell color solid which is irregular in form and varies with the particular pigments or colorants being represented.*

Pope originally thought of his color solid as accurate in terms of visually equal spacing (proportional to geometric spacing), but he came to realize that this was not so. No color solid has ever been successful in achieving that objective, now thought by many to be unobtainable.[20] However, the distances between pairs of points within the Pope solid is at least roughly proportional to the visual differences between the colors represented by those points.

The Pope solid is perhaps the only color solid[21] ever designed primarily to show the nature of first-order trends in color appearance—free of the confusion of second-order and minor variations.†

In terms of its objectives the Pope color solid is remarkably revealing, especially when it comes to relating hues of high intensity with their characteristic darknesses. In consequence, it can be of particular value to those who may wish to acquire, with minimum confusion and effort, a basic understanding of color "dimensions" and color relationships.

*For a more detailed discussion of the features of the Pope system, as compared with the Munsell system, see the Supplement, pp. 110-112.

†For a discussion of second-order variations, see the Supplement, pp. 106-110.

Color in Art

James M. Carpenter

The exhibition *Color in Art* is based on the premise that an understanding of color relationships contributes to the better understanding of art. Since the same faculties of color perception that yield heightened experiences in the presence of works of art also enable us to classify and relate colors for purposes of constructing a conceptual color world, a parallel study seems natural. It is appropriate that such an exhibition, possibly the first of its kind, be held at Harvard where the basic ideas of this particular theoretical approach were established.

In order to discuss color in works of art in the manner proposed here it is essential to use terms in a quite specific way and to explain relationships with comparable specificity. In particular, to understand the presentation of ideas one should follow the exhibition in its proper sequence, as well as following the sequence in the catalogue. It is especially important that the reader, or viewer, understand the character of the three-dimensional concept of the color world, which Arthur Pope called a color solid. While the color solid will be summarily described in this section, a much fuller explication is contained in the Supplements. The color charts on pages 15, 18, 22, and 26 provide the best way to gain familiarity with this arrangement of color. The three-dimensional models in the exhibition, and the diagrams of them here, will assist further in establishing the form of the solid. Both the Introduction to Color and the Supplement on the Pope Color Solid should be referred to as much as necessary.

Both Arthur Pope and his teacher Denman Ross believed that an understanding of orderly relationships in color and the discrimination it took to perceive these were basic to the critical perception of paintings. Denman Ross was a collector and a painter; his extraordinary judgment is apparent in the number of fine works of European and Asiatic art in the Boston Museum of Fine Arts that are part of the Ross Collection. Arthur Pope is also remembered by his students and colleagues as an authority in matters of artistic judgment, and during his long career as a teacher he passed on to hundreds of students some of his sense of quality in art. While most of his basic ideas appeared in his books and articles, it was his clarifying explanation of what he saw in a drawing or painting that students remembered best. Ross's ideas were his starting point, together with those of Charles Herbert Moore who taught drawing and painting at Harvard, but Arthur Pope filled out and made more systematic "the theory of representation and design."[1]

It has not been popular to be an art theorist in the twentieth century. To modern historical thinking theories smack of rules and academicism. Arthur Pope was emphatically opposed to this kind of "art theory." He grew up in the period of latter-day Impressionism when many artists learned to paint by rules (for example, the banning of black from the palette) and he recognized the superficiality of such rules. Yet he was very sensitive to the presence of order in a work of art. Not *a* theory of art but *the* theory of visual organization in art is what interested him. While he was intensely aware of the role of intuition in art and frequently referred to the mysterious role of the creative imagination, he felt that this aspect of art was not capable of rational analysis. Visual organization was—and he came close to equating art and order, as Ross had done. Order, Pope recognized, can be achieved intuitively as well as consciously and he often termed it "emotionally appreciable order" to distinguish it from the measurable order that appeals more to the intellect.

While Pope's theoretical studies were primarily directed to the understanding of art ("as we have to learn a language before we can understand what is written in it"), he always relied heavily on studio practice to give precision to visual observations. He himself was a most sensitive painter and his students all drew and painted as part of their training. Principles of drawing, representation, and design were all explored with pencil and watercolor in the introductory course known for many years as Fine Arts 1A. The color charts executed for this course had to be precisely judged by the student to satisfy Pope. Sloppy thinking was not encouraged; he believed that making artistic judgments was just as demanding as making mathematical judgments. "It is only when we can understand or 'read' a painting clearly and thoroughly that we are in a position to judge and appreciate it as to its artistic value."

Many people had the superficial impression that since students drew and painted in Pope's classes they were being trained to be artists. This was not his primary aim. He was rather like a musician who conducts a "master class" with the idea of discovering in a composition all the richness and refinements it has to offer. He simply believed that by actually drawing and painting one could intensify the experience of seeing and understanding. He was not sure his students would grasp clearly enough what he meant when he spoke of "uniformity of color attraction," for example, unless they had actually executed a composition with uniform color attractions.

The connection between the ordering of color and the practice of painting led both Ross and Pope to continue use of the traditional 12-hue color circle, an arrangement which corresponded most closely with the way their pigments mixed on the palette, that is subtractively. The arrangement based on 10 hues used by Munsell was determined by the mixing of complementaries through spinning, that is additively. (Other differences between the Munsell and Pope systems are explained in the Supplement.)

The planning of this exhibition closely followed the substance of Arthur Pope's teaching and writing. In only a few places here have his terms been altered: the most notable innovation is the computerized diagram, or color score, evolved by Howard T. Fisher, which has received Pope's enthusiastic endorsement. The value of the three-dimensional concept, as Pope always claimed, is as an aid to clear thinking about color. Apart from its graphic display of first-order trends in color appearance, the Pope solid also records ratios of contrasts among colors: a small contrast is registered as a short distance between points within the color solid, a strong color contrast is registered by a long distance between points. Or, as Pope expressed it, "Lines drawn from point to point in the solid represent with approximate accuracy the contrasts made by the corresponding tones when juxtaposed on a flat surface."

No color system using distance coordinates is able to take account of an important basic fact of color—the variability in color perception. Identical colors can be made to look unlike each other and colors that are actually different can be made to look the same, as Josef Albers has dramatically demonstrated. Nevertheless an orderly model of the color world, particularly if it is familiar enough so that it becomes a mental construct, can assist us in seeing color relationships in painting and especially in communicating in an area in which verbal language alone is inadequate.

ORGANIZING COLOR BY LIMITING COLOR RANGE

Since Pope's approach to color leans heavily on graphic means of analyzing color relationships, we may begin by exploring a painting, Philip Guston's *Summer, 1954* (no. 1), with the help of the color score seen in figure 1. The derivation of this computer-produced diagram from the color solid is explained in detail in "Transforming and Scaling the Color Solid," in the Supplement. In brief, the color score records relationships among the three attributes of color: value (or darkness), hue, and intensity.* The color score identifies several relationships that we can see in the painting, mostly relationships of limitation:

1. There are no strong lights or darks in the painting: the value range is limited to about half the complete range from white to black.
2. There are two dominant hue areas: warm hues in the orange-to-red range and cool hues in the yellow-greens. Other hues are subordinate: yellows, red-purples, blue-purples, blues, and blue-greens. Purple and yellow-orange are absent.
3. Intensity is greatest for the red-orange, slightly less for red and yellow-green, and low for other hues.

*I use here the term *value* since it is widely adopted by art critics and writers about art to refer to light and dark relationships. Professor Fisher prefers the term *darkness,* and uses it in his sections of this volume.

1
Philip Guston (1913-   )
Summer, 1954
Oil on canvas, 60 x 60½ inches
Anonymous Loan, 1.1971

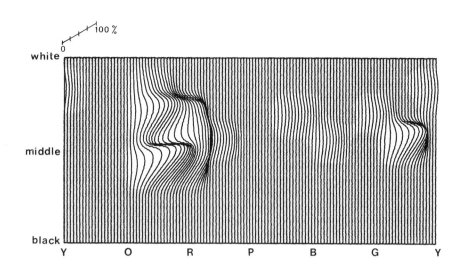

Figure 1
Color score of Philip Guston's Summer, *1954. Value is recorded vertically; white at the top, black at the bottom. Hue is recorded horizontally; reading from left to right: yellow, orange, red, purple, blue, green, yellow. Intensity is recorded obliquely by the degree of "relief" out from the background; higher relief means greater intensity. The toned areas represent the absence of hues in the painting.*

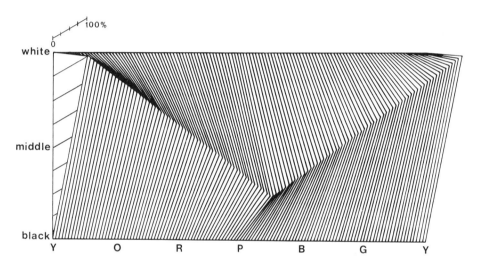

Figure 2
Color score of the exterior surface of the color solid showing the oblique edges of all the hue triangles (including many more than the basic 12). The absence of vertical lines indicates that no neutrals are recorded here except for white and black. Since only colors of maximum intensity are recorded, a comparison with figure 1 reveals either Guston's omission of hues or his use of hues at lesser intensities.

To see the degree and the kind of color limitation in Guston's painting compare figure 1 with figure 2, which is the color score of the complete range of colors at their highest intensities, plus white and black.

The Guston painting and its color score introduce one of the central principles of color organization—limited ranges. In the broader context of design, or artistic form, the perception of similarity is a common type of visual organization: for example, the recurrence of shapes (angularity, circularity, and so on), of directions, of size (or scale) in works of art. In a sense these are also limited ranges selected from all possible shapes or directions or sizes. Their similarity or relative uniformity constitutes the order and imparts to them some artistic form. Relatedness of this kind in color is just as much a part of design as relatedness in shape, direction, or size.

Besides uniformity (exact or approximate) other leading principles of design are sequence (regular change) and balance (left and right equilibrium). These are also felt in color as in shape, direction, and size. The faculties that enter into

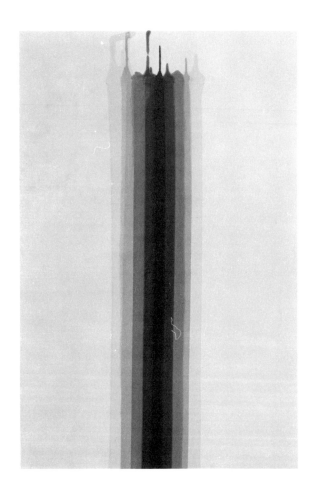

3
Edward Hopper (1882-1967)
Libby House, Portland, Maine, 1927
Watercolor, 14 x 20 inches
Purchase: Louise E. Bettens Fund,
1927.257

2
Morris Louis (1912-1962)
Color Barrier, 1961
Acrylic resin paint (Magna) on canvas,
91⅜ x 60 inches
Purchase: Louise E. Bettens Fund,
1963.105

4
Charles E. Burchfield (1893-1967)
August Sunlight, 1916
Watercolor, 13½ x 19½ inches
Purchase: Louise E. Bettens Fund,
1930.463

our perception of color in works of art are the same that enable us to classify color. The starting point of a psychological color system is our perception of uniformities and of regular changes.

Referring to color charts 2, 3, and 4 (pp. 18, 22, 26) we may draw the following conclusions about the presence of these types of order:

1. There is *uniformity* (constancy) of hue within each of the twelve triangles; of value (or darkness), along any horizontal line in a hue triangle, or throughout any one of the horizontal cross-sections of the color solid; of intensity, along any vertical line in each of the twelve triangles, or from any of the concentric cylinders within the color solid.
2. There is *regular change* (gradation), in reference to the three-dimensional solid: of hue, along any horizontally changing line within the color solid; of value, along any vertically changing line within the color solid; and of intensity, along any line that moves toward or away from the central axis.

Further details about the exact nature of the three-dimensional diagram of the color world are to be found in the Supplement. At this time the color solid can be summarized as follows: It is made up of twelve hue triangles joined by their common neutral axis. Since the high intensity colors occur at different value levels the bounding line of high intensities rises and falls as it travels around the circular outer limits of the solid. A vertical slice through the center of the solid shows two roughly complementary hue triangles, like red and green, orange and blue. A horizontal slice or cross-section shows all twelve hues and all of the intensities achievable at that value level.

Another recent abstract painting, Morris Louis's *Color Barrier* (no. 2), is much more restricted in color than the painting by Guston. It is virtually a three-hue painting, with the near-neutral canvas and near-neutral dark green center providing contrasts in value. Other contrasts come from the intensity of the orange and the wide differences in value.

In representational painting, as in abstract painting, color organization through limitation of range is common. Edward Hopper's *Libby House, Portland, Maine* (no. 3) and Charles Burchfield's *August Sunlight* (no. 4) are limited in hues and intensities, with different hue regions dominant in each. Burchfield's watercolor is particularly interesting because of his notations on the painting itself ("neut. blue; YG and white"). The region from orange through yellow to green is developed while all reds and purples are omitted.

The color scores of the watercolors *Simplon Pass* (no. 5) by J. M. W. Turner and *Canoe in the Rapids* (no. 6) by Winslow Homer reveal some of their significant differences. The Turner painting possesses three dominant hues—a red, a

5
J. M. W. Turner (1775-1851)
Simplon Pass, ca. 1841
Watercolor on paper, 21 x 28 inches
Gift of Edward W. Forbes, 1954.133

6
Winslow Homer (1836-1910)
Canoe in the Rapids, 1897
Watercolor, 13½ x 20½ inches (sight)
Purchase: Louise E. Bettens Fund,
1924.30

Figure 3
Color score of J. M. W. Turner's
Simplon Pass.

Figure 4
Color score of Winslow Homer's
Canoe in the Rapids.

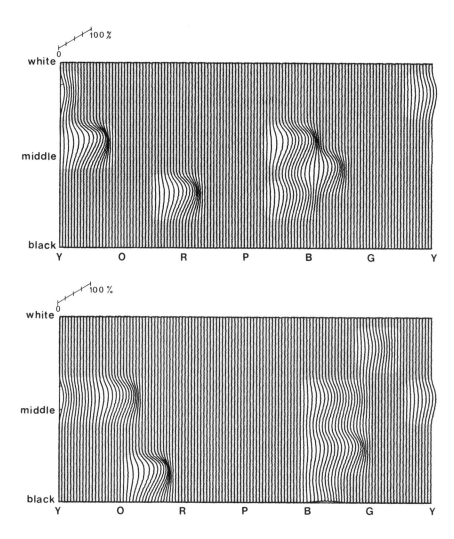

Figure 5
Hue and intensity diagram of J.M.W.
Turner's Simplon Pass.

Figure 6
Hue and intensity diagram of Winslow
Homer's Canoe in the Rapids.

Another way of diagramming the hue
and intensity ranges used by the two
artists. Value relations are not recorded
at all in these diagrams, which are de-
rived from the cylindrical bounding
shape of the color solid projected to the
ground plane as a circle. These diagrams
register the presence of many near-
neutrals (shaded centers) in both paint-
ings, which the color scores do not
indicate as clearly.

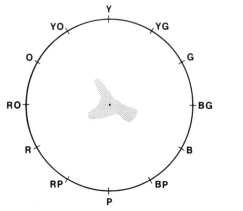

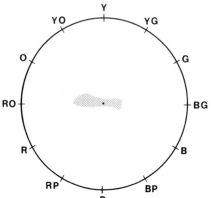

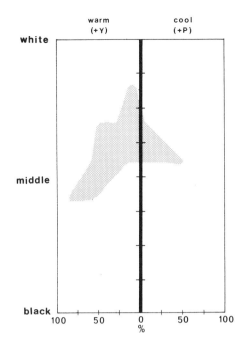

white

warm
(+Y)

cool
(+P)

middle

black

100   50   0   50   100

%

Figure 7

Value and intensity diagram of Philip Guston's Summer, 1954. *Except for a warm-cool separation, value and intensity are recorded without regard for hue. Warm hue triangles (Y-RP) are imagined as flattened into a single plane to the left of the neutral axis and cool hue triangles (YG-P) into the same plane to the right of the axis. For the Guston painting the diagram records the limitation of value range, as does the color score in figure 1. Less than half the total white to black range is used. A large number of both warm and cool colors fall within the shaded area.*

yellow-orange, and a blue, each quite distinct in hue as revealed by the horizontal spacing between the rippled hue lines on figure 3. Two active hue regions are revealed in figure 4, the color score of the Homer: the orange to red and the blue to green. Compared with the Turner there is little intensity in the yellowish oranges and purplish blues. The degree of selectivity practiced by both artists is made clear in the relatively few hue lines (verticals) that have some degree of intensity (variation from vertical). In general Turner's colors are more intense than those of Homer. The commingling of the different hues in both paintings, particularly in the neutral areas, is not clearly presented in the color score, so at this point two new diagrams must be introduced.

The diagram of hues and intensities (figs. 5 and 6) is a plan of color space and therefore circular in shape, resembling the chart of the hue circle. As a plan of the three-dimensional model, its circumference stands for high intensity colors, its interior area stands for varying lesser intensities, and the center for neutral. Values are not differentiated here but hues and intensities can be accurately located. Furthermore, it is simple to use as a practical tool, unlike the computerized color scores which cannot be casually produced. For the Turner and Homer watercolors the diagrams record the facts that there are many rather neutral colors, warm and cool, that make up the total color range of the Homer (shaded area), and that the three hue regions with a mixture of two in the neutral-purple area dominate in the Turner.

A third type of diagram registers values and intensities without regard to hue, except for a broad distinction between warm and cool. The diagram of values and intensities is arrived at by flattening the twelve hue triangles into a plane. For a painting like Philip Guston's *Summer, 1954* (no. 1), the shaded area of its diagram records the fact that there are many mixtures among the warms, among the cools, and, in the neutral area, among the warms and the cools (see fig. 7).

The Relative Nature of Color Perception

As we move further into matters of color relationships in painting, emphasis should be given to the relative nature of color perception. Ever since Chevreul's work in color theory, and centuries earlier in the practice of artists, the relative nature of color has been recognized. Since the 1940s it has become the specialized interest of Josef Albers. His research into what he terms the "interaction of color" has produced astonishing results of a "fool the eye" nature.[2]

Most of Albers' examples of color interaction are extensions of what Chevreul identified as *simultaneous contrast,* or the tendency of one color sensation to generate its opposite. These opposites refer us back again to the basic attributes of hue, value, and intensity: warm versus cool, light versus dark, and intense

versus neutral. The opposite effect from simultaneous contrast is termed a *spreading effect*. When colors thread through each other rather than being juxtaposed in relatively large areas the sensation of one spreads over another, a light color making its surroundings lighter, a warm making its surroundings warmer, and so on.

A silk-screen print, *Inward Eye* (no. 7), by Richard Anuszkiewicz, a student of Albers, illustrates these effects: looked at up close the intensities enhance each other by simultaneous contrast; looked at from some distance the warms diminish the intensities of the cools and the cools diminish the intensities of the warms. From a normal viewing distance both optical effects vie for the dominant role.

These situations of color relativity point up the fact that when dealing with works of art, in which colors are always influencing each other, a method of classification that emphasizes absoluteness is not particularly useful. A system that deals with rigid steps for the specification of color matching is hardly adaptable to understanding color relations that depend on relative redness or yellowness, intensity or neutrality. Pope's color space is a conceptual tool that can be equally applied to paintings done in different media or seen in normal variations of lighting. A painting is a self-sufficient complex of color with an internal organization that invites our understanding. We analyze this organization by means of the way we perceive similarities, contrasts, and regular changes, in a relativistic context.

Limited Range of Hue and Intensity

The limited color ranges found in the Turner and Homer paintings are part of their formal organization. Limitation or restriction of color range, as a kind of general uniformity or constancy, is to be differentiated from precise uniformity— i.e., identical hues or values or intensities—which is not often found in works of art. Much more frequent, and more interesting, is the *relative* sameness of a color region.

"Analogous hues" have long been recognized as providing a unifying effect. Rubens' *Quos Ego* or *The Wrath of Neptune* (no. 8) is the clearest illustration here of the use of a restricted hue range with the warm colors dominant. In Turner's *Simplon Pass* (no. 5) there are three hue areas, two warm and one cool, but neither warm nor cool dominates. Furthermore they are joined, as the diagram of hues and intensities shows, by a region of mixtures of these two. In Homer's *Canoe in the Rapids* (no. 6), a number of hues are recognizable, but most of them are at low intensities. In all three paintings, however, we sense the essential similarity of the color organization. The important principle of this kind of color organization, then, is not simply the dominance of a single hue

7
Richard Anuszkiewicz (1930-   )
Inward Eye, ca. 1970
Silk-screen print, 25⅜ x 19⁹⁄₁₆ inches
Colby College, Museum Purchase

8

Peter Paul Rubens (1577-1640)

Quos Ego or *The Wrath of Neptune,*
ca. 1635

Oil on panel, 19¼ x 25¼ inches

Purchase: Alpheus Hyatt Fund, 1942.174

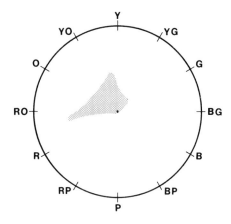

Figure 8
Hue and intensity diagram of Rubens'
The Wrath of Neptune. *The strongest*
color accents in the red to red-orange
and yellow regions are shown, as is the
absence of all blues and purples. The
greens in the water are extremely
neutralized.

region but the limitation of hue and intensity range. Such limitation has been a favorite with painters in the Western tradition since the Renaissance because it is usually accompanied by an unrestricted value range. A tradition that embraced strong modeling or emphatic light needed a full value range to create these effects.

The controlling power of the hue and intensity limitation found in Rubens' *Quos Ego* is symbolized in figure 8. The hues are restricted to the red-yellow-neutral region with the addition of a neutralized green in the water. By preparing the ground with a warm tone Rubens established the basic tonality in the yellow-orange region. As he dragged his neutrals over this, in the clouds, water, and horses, he set up a cool-warm contrast that permeates the whole painting. In characteristic Baroque fashion he dispersed several unitary accents

9
Rajput School

Krishna and Attendants in Chariot,
from a Bwagarata Purana, ca. 1540
Tempera on paper, 6⅞ x 8¾ inches
Private Collection, Cambridge, Mass.

10
Bukhara School
Two Figures and a Tree, ca. 1560
Tempera on paper, 10⅜ x 5⅜ inches
Gift of John Goelet, formerly in the
Collection of Louis J. Cartier, 1958.74

11
Persian School, Qazuin
Youth with Bow and Arrows, ca. 1580
Tempera on paper, 10⅝ x 7 inches
Gift of John Goelet, formerly in the
Collection of Louis J. Cartier, 1958.78a

12
Ammi Phillips (1788-1865)
Portrait of Harriet Leavens, ca. 1815
Oil on canvas, 56¼ x 27 inches
Gift of the Estate of Harriet Anna Niel,
1945.27

13
Robert Indiana (1928-   )
Art (Red, Blue, and Green Art), 1970
Oil on canvas, 24 x 24 inches
Colby College, Museum Purchase

over the picture: a yellow accent at the sunburst near the horizon, a dark neutral in the right foreground, a white or light neutral on the horses and a red around Neptune. Several subordinate recurrences of these four terminal colors are found amid their many mixtures. Sharp contrasts, like those at Neptune's face or the horses' bodies merge with sustained gradations of value and hue to contribute to the richness of the whole.

In other traditions of painting, limited value ranges play an equally important role. They are, in turn, usually accompanied by relatively unrestricted hues and intensities. Since the dominant effect of limitation in values is to produce a flat or plane surface, such color organization is common in decorative art where the preservation of a flat surface is in order. The three Asian miniatures in the exhibition (nos. 9-11), or the example of American folk art, a portrait by Ammi Phillips (no. 12), all have large areas of color that are held together by limiting the value differences, a technique also found in the Guston painting (no. 1). Usually we are not much aware of such restrictions until we direct conscious attention to them, as in imagining the introduction of a sharp white or black into the Guston painting. The modern tradition of decorative color, which often limits value contrasts while allowing intensities and hues to come out strongly was initiated by artists like Gauguin and Matisse and is still vital in the age of Robert Indiana whose painting *Art* (no. 13) employs three intense colors of nearly identical values.

DECORATIVE COLOR

A broad distinction can be made between the use of color in painting primarily for decorative purposes and its use to create an illusion of space, form, and light: decorative color versus representational color, as the distinction could be stated, or two-dimensional color versus three-dimensional color. Many master colorists, like Rubens or Cézanne, incorporated both qualities into their paintings: In *Quos Ego* (no. 8) the strong contrasts of Neptune and the horses in the foreground hold these forms in front of the boats and clouds, but the tonal contrasts and the general activity throughout the background establish a surface coherence in that plane. The result is a readable sequence of many planes, with color that is basically two-plane in its effect. Decorative and representational color coexist in a stimulating tension.

Matisse's later paintings, or the silk-screen prints from his book *Jazz,* are brilliant examples of decorative color, usually identifiable in *Jazz* as two-plane color since the effect is that of flat-colored areas placed against a background.

14
Henri Matisse (1869-1954)
Plate V from *Jazz: Le Cheval,
l'Ecuyère et le Clown*, 1947
Pochoir, 16½ x 25½ inches
M12,161

15
Henri Matisse (1869-1954)
Plate VIII from *Jazz: Icare*, 1947
Pochoir, 16½ x 12¾ inches
M12,164

In some examples from the *Jazz* series (nos. 14 and 15), we can speak of one-plane color, since no particular color area remains as background but all insist on becoming figures against another colored ground. The effect is often ambiguous: in the page "Icare" (no. 15) the yellow stars are clearly read as on the blue while the black figure reads ambiguously as behind and as in front of the blue. In part this depends on what part of the figure we are observing; the red "heart" pushes the upper part of the black figure into the further plane while the lower figure reads as in front of the blue. Our interest is quite wonderfully divided among the four colors—neither blue, nor black, nor yellow, nor red is allowed to slip away from our attention for even an instant.

Some of the recent masters of ambiguous color planes are to be found among the op-artists of the 1960s. Richard Anuszkiewicz' silk-screen print *Inward Eye* (no. 7), is a typical example of modern color sophistication. In addition to the presence of both simultaneous contrast and spreading effect, the print displays the use of one-plane color or ambiguous-plane color, depending on how your eyes are operating at a given moment. Beyond that, the print is composed of five vertical strips with very regular sequences in all three attributes of color. The background strips grade from light blue-purple to dark green, with increasing intensities. The centers grade from yellow to red with more or less constant intensities and at the same values as the backgrounds. The warm-cool juxtaposition at constant values produces the effect of vibration that is favored by op-artists, but it is the superbly adjusted gradations and value constancies that provide the basic color structure of the print.

Gradations are important in the small *Landscape* (no. 16), an early work of Marsden Hartley. Yellow fuses with green and into red, creating orderly sequences. At the same time this painting is a good example of decorative color in the way it is equally animated throughout. Its upper half possesses a greater variety of hues while its lower half contains larger areas and stronger value contrasts. The result is an equal visual attraction in all parts of the painting and a strong sense of picture surface.

Here again, the principle of general uniformity or sameness is apparent, but now uniformity is that of *attraction*. This seems to be the key principle of successful decorative color. The great examples of Byzantine mosaics and twelfth- and thirteenth-century stained glass set the standards of high achievement in monumental decorative color; in all of them the artists held under control the two major variables of contrast and size. When the contrasts between colors were strong or the intensities high within single colors, the sizes of the areas were kept relatively small. Larger areas were given either less contrast with their surroundings or more neutral coloring. The variations were infinite within these general controls.

16

Marsden Hartley (1877-1943)

Landscape

Oil on board, 11½ x 11½ inches (sight)

Gift of James N. Rosenberg,
1958.304

17
Pablo Picasso (1881-1973)
Abstraction III, ca. 1920
Stencil, 12⅜ x 8⅛ inches
Gift of Arthur Pope, M10,970

18
Pablo Picasso (1881-1973)
Abstraction IV, ca. 1920
Stencil, 11¼ x 8⅞ inches
Gift of Arthur Pope, M10,971

19
Maurice Brazil Prendergast (1861-1924)
Beach, New England, 1920
Watercolor over graphite, 15¼ x 22⅛ inches
Gift of Mrs. Charles Prendergast, 1961.137

20
Henri de Toulouse-Lautrec (1864-1901)
Trapeze Artist at the Medrano Circus, 1893
Gouache on cardboard, 31⅜ x 23⅞ inches
Bequest of Annie Swan Coburn, 1934.34

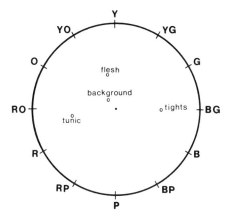

Figure 9
Hue and intensity diagram of Toulouse-Lautrec's Trapeze Artist. *The main color areas have been planned in relation to the brownish background. In the original painting the three major local colors —flesh, tunic, and tights—are all approximately equidistant from the background. In hue and intensity contrast, the tights are furthest but they are closest in value. In a three-dimensional model, therefore, the linear distances would come out about equal, just as the visual distances do in the painting.*

Many variables make up visual attraction; beside contrast, inherent intensity, and size, there are psychological attractions, textures, details, and variety of shapes. Picasso used a number of variables in his stencil prints (nos. 17 and 18). His colors are much less intense than Matisse's in *Jazz,* but they also achieve an equilibrium through overall equal attraction. *Abstraction IV* (no. 18) has a blue that can be read in four different planes across the top of the picture, yet it constantly exerts an influence to be read as in one plane.

Prendergast was a witty exponent of decorative color: in the watercolor shown, *Beach, New England* (no. 19), the weakest area of the picture, as color, is the solidest form represented, a stone wall. The color areas in Toulouse-Lautrec's *Trapeze Artist* (no. 20) are all roughly equidistant in terms of attraction from the brown background tone—again an instance of decorative color. This is clear from the hue and intensity diagram shown in figure 9.

Vuillard's four-color lithograph *L'Atre* (no. 21) balances the size of an area against its intensity. The neutrals have the largest areas, the yellow and green, both about half intensity, are in lesser amounts, and the intense red is smallest. The control in Bonnard's *Rue Vue d'en Haut* (no. 22) stems partly from the equality of contrast of a darker green and a lighter yellow-orange against a red-tinged neutral.

REPRESENTATIONAL COLOR

The Illusion of Space

When color is used for the opposite purpose, that is, to enhance or reinforce spatial effects, there are again usually a few simple principles at work but seemingly infinite variation in their application. Greater contrasts come forward, especially if supported by the drawing of the forms, as in the Rubens (no. 8). High intensities, a kind of contrast, also tend to come forward. Warm colors will often come forward more positively than cool colors, though there are many conditions that will counteract this effect: in the Rubens the value contrasts in the neutral horses easily keep them in front of Neptune's red robe. But in Guston's painting (no. 1), where value contrasts are less, the warm colors tend to float forward as compared with the cools.

Winslow Homer's *Canoe in the Rapids* (no. 6) has a convincing sequence of planes near the center of the picture. Black accents are used in the foreground only: intensities are strongest in the canoeist nearer to us; modeling is much weaker in the farther canoeist than the nearer one; and the contrast between the nearer man and the background of sky and trees is greater than between the further one and his background. It is apparent that Homer, like most good colorists, relies more on color than on perspective for his major spatial effects.

Degas, in his earlier works, was fascinated by the way that color contrasts could produce the illusion of increasing distance from the observer. *At the Races* (no. 23) combines the effect of sunlight breaking through dark clouds with that of spatial recession. The darkened atmosphere of the distance is the tone toward which all local colors move, and their distance into this depth is given by the degree to which they approach this tone.

The Illusion of Light

When we proceed from the way color enhances space to the way it enhances light we move into a very special province of color. As the Impressionists demonstrated, color can be virtually synonymous with light. The treatment of color that results in the illusion of light begins, historically, with the Flemish painters of the fifteenth century, who first analyzed the changes that take place when a given local color is seen in differing degrees of light. They were not theoreticians and did not publish their results in treatises the way the Italians did with their discoveries in perspective. But Jan van Eyck's empirical exploration of color did result in the discovery that when light falls from one general source upon objects with varying local colors, these local colors are modified very systematically. At the same time that the Italians were discovering that systematic perspective created a new sense of wholeness in the rendering of objects in space, the Flemish were discovering that systematic modification of local colors created a new sense of wholeness in the rendering of objects in light.

Their discoveries were of two related phenomena. First, when light on a given local color (i.e., object-color) is reduced, usually by modeling as the surface of the form turns away from the light, the value lowers and the intensity reduces. While the color gradually becomes less intense as it darkens in shadow, the hue remains the same, unless affected by colored light from another object or light source. Second, when several local colors are turning away from the light and into shadow, their values and intensities change according to the same ratio. There is, therefore, a *proportional diminution of value and intensity contrasts.* This produces a color organization that is felt both as an inherent ordering of color and as the creation of a convincing illusion of light. Again the parallel with perspective and space comes to mind: linear perspective results in an ordered system of lines and planes at the same time that it creates an illusion of space.

Since van Eyck, all painters who have sought effects of light with color have been responsive to this principle in nature. Vermeer is the classic example of an artist who is supremely sensitive to the proportional relations of colors in varying lights, and Arthur Pope used Vermeer's paintings to explain the "mode of total visual effect," which will be discussed later.

21
Edouard Vuillard (1868-1940)
L'Arte, from "Paysages et Intérieurs,"
1899
Color lithograph, 13¼ x 10⅞ inches
M13,610

22
Pierre Bonnard (1867-1947)
Rue Vue d'en Haut, from "Quelques
Aspects de la Vie de Paris," 1899
Color lithograph, 14½ x 8¾ inches
M13,701

23
Edgar Degas (1834-1917)
At the Races: They're Off! ca. 1870
Oil on canvas, 12 x 18½ inches
Bequest of Annie S. Coburn, 1934.30

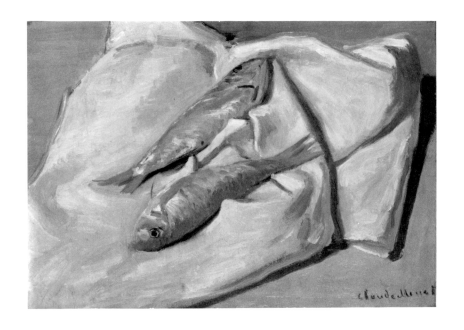

24

Claude Monet (1840-1926)

Fish, ca. 1870

Oil on canvas, 14 x 19¾ inches

Gift of Friends of the Fogg Art Museum,
1925.16

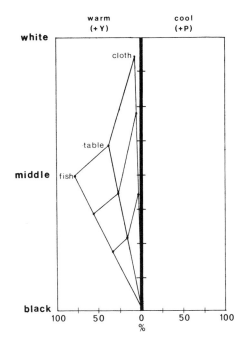

warm
(+Y)

cool
(+P)

white

cloth

table

middle

fish

black

100   50   0   50   100
%

Figure 10
Hue and intensity diagram of Claude Monet's Fish. *The proportional diminution in value and intensity contrasts is recorded as the three local colors—the red-orange of the fish, the yellow-orange of the table, and the near-neutral of the cloth—model toward black as they turn into shadow. Contrasts are strongest in light, less in half-light, and least in shadow.*

Claude Monet was as precise as Vermeer in his observation of color in nature, and his painting *Fish* (no. 24) is a good example of this precision. It is simple enough so that we can analyze its components with the aid of a diagram of values and intensities (fig. 10). Three local colors are plotted on the diagram and since they are all warm they fall to the left of the neutral axis. The cloth is very nearly neutral. As they go into shadow (a modeling shadow on the cloth and a cast shadow on the table) each darkens and loses intensity proportionally. The table starts darker and therefore arrives at a darker shadow. Where the shadow side of the cloth receives light from the table the resultant tone is a mixture of the neutral of the cloth and the colored light from the table. In a similar way the shadow side of the fish is modified by neutral light from the cloth. The fish, being shiny, picks up highlights—mixtures of the light source and the local color of the fish. The basic principle of a proportional diminution of contrasts, then, is modified by (1) colored light, received either from another object or another source, and (2) reflections, as the shiny surface of an object reflects other objects or a light source.

Edward Hopper's watercolor *Highland Light* (no. 25) emphasizes the reflection of the sun off almost all sunlit surfaces, forcing the local colors toward white or near white. The chief clues to local colors are therefore in the shadows. But these in turn are highly modified by the sky color or ground color and go toward blue or purple if the former and yellow if the latter. This is the heritage of Impressionist color, which we will examine later.

VALUE RELATIONS IN PAINTING. A major problem of the landscape artist is that of coping with the limited range of values in his paints in relation to the broader value range of nature. He has hit upon various solutions to this problem. One of the most difficult to achieve successfully is, surprisingly, the *proportional transcription of value relations* from nature. To achieve the desired illusion with this means requires highly precise powers of observation, and the most successful have been artists like Vermeer, Corot, and, again, the young Monet. Monet's *Route de la Ferme St. Simeon, Honfleur* (no. 26) is such an example. An overcast day with a tinge of blueness in the sky results in nearly shadowless figures and trees. A slight accumulation of cast shadow under the trees darkens the snow gently and turns it toward blue, but our interest now is with the value relations. Given the conditions of light it seems that Monet has scaled off all his values from the white of the lightest snow to the foreground blacks in exactly the same proportion as in nature. A convincing "relational model of nature," as E. H. Gombrich has termed it, is the result.[3]

The Dutch Baroque artists, following the lead of Caravaggio, developed the technique of sliding values downward with an increasing compression of con-

25
Edward Hopper (1882-1967)
Highland Light, 1930
Watercolor, 15⅝ x 24½ inches
Purchase: Louise E. Bettens Fund,
1930.462

26

Claude Monet (1840-1926)

Route de la Ferme St. Simeon, Honfleur,
ca. 1867

Oil on canvas, 21½ x 31¼ inches

Bequest of Grenville L. Winthrop,
1943.260

27
Jacob van Ruisdael (ca. 1630-1682)
A Road Lined with Trees, ca. 1675
Oil on canvas, 25⅜ x 20⅞ inches
Bequest of Edwin H. Abbott, 1966.168

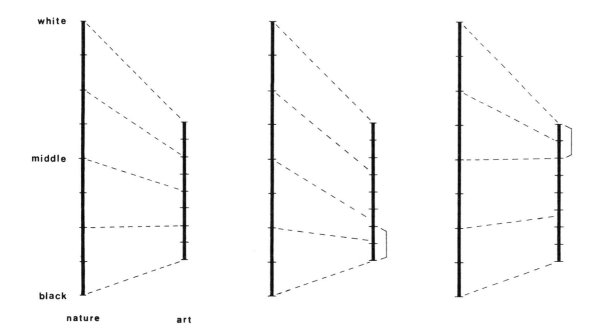

white

middle

black

nature   art

Figure 11
In translating the white to black range in nature into painting, darkness relations may be proportional, as at the left; *crowded in the dark region,* in the middle; or *crowded in the light region,* at the right. *Crowding of the darks allows contrasts within the lights to approach closer to those of nature, while crowding of the lights gives a wider range to the darks in the painting.*

trasts in the darks (fig. 11). *Crowding of the darks* results in stronger contrasts in the lights, as in Jacob van Ruisdael's *A Road Lined with Trees* (no. 27), enhancing the luminosity of the sky and sunlit regions. Later, photographers discovered similar effects by underexposing their negatives. Turner's *Simplon Pass* (no. 5) illustrates a third solution, a *crowding of the lights.* Values are systematically moved up so that large areas are close to the white paper, and yet small dark accents are retained for contrast.

INTENSITY RELATIONS IN PAINTING. Intensities can also be systematically adjusted either to enhance light effect or to achieve some desired inherent organization of color. Again a *proportional transcription of intensities* may be considered a norm, and this is well illustrated by Alfred Sisley's *Le Pont de Conflans à Moret* (no. 28). The colors in the grass are carried over into the painting with intensities that seem to have the same relation to the value scale of the painting as real grass has to the wider value range of nature.

Turner's watercolor of *Ehrenbreitstein* (no. 29), on the other hand, systematically *suppresses the intensity range.* Colors are hardly more than renderings of relative coolness and warmth, standing for what in nature would be a wider intensity range. The warmth in the background conveys the sense of the sun breaking through dark clouds, but the shaded foreground trees, for instance, have no hint of green to relieve their neutrality. Surprisingly, one becomes so adapted to the reduced range that a considerable effect of color emerges from the whole. Paul Signac's watercolor *La Rochelle* (no. 30) shows the *exaggeration of intensities,* with a nearly full range of hues from red-orange through the yellows and greens to blue, all at high intensities and with many admixtures of white, either as paper or paint. In figure 12 the three methods of treating intensity relations are shown diagramatically.

28
Alfred Sisley (1839-1899)
Le Pont de Conflans à Moret, 1872
Oil on canvas, 18⁹⁄₁₆ x 21¹³⁄₁₆ inches
Gift of Grenville L. Winthrop,
1942.206

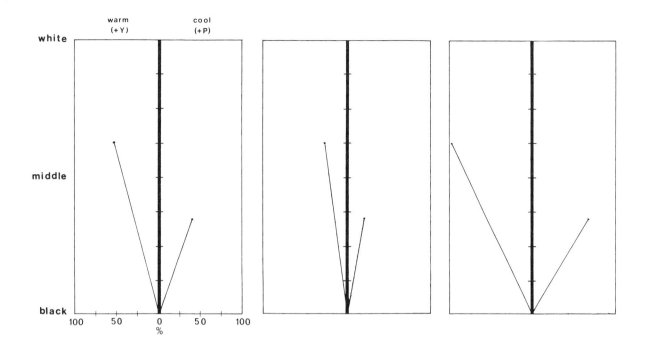

warm
(+Y) cool
(+P)

white

middle

black

100 50 0 50 100
%

Figure 12
Intensity relations may be systematically varied in translating from nature into painting. Left: *the value and intensity diagram records the way two colors, a warm and a cool, might model into shadow in nature. It could also stand for the proportional transcription of this into painting.* Middle: *the diagram illustrates a suppression of intensities (as in Turner's* Ehrenbreitstein). Right: *the diagram shows an exaggeration of intensities compared with relation of these two colors in nature.*

29
J. M. W. Turner (1775-1851)
Ehrenbreitstein, ca. 1822
Watercolor, 7¾ x 12½ inches
Gift of Edward W. Forbes, 1904.35

More is involved in these choices than the desire to find a way to capture light. Turner's suppression of intensity, growing out of the near-monochrome watercolors of earlier English painters, reflects a desire to exploit the unifying power of a strictly limited palette, while Signac's exaggeration recognizes another kind of unification: that of uniform high intensities. The use of only high-intensity colors mixed with white results in a coherence due to the elimination of grays, blacks, or mixtures with these. Stated differently, virtually all colors are taken from the upper surface of the color solid and none from the inside or lower surface.

POPE'S FOUR MODES OF REPRESENTATION

Essential to an understanding of color in art is the apprehension of its role in relation to all other aspects of a particular work of art. Most color theorists arrived at certain ideas of "harmony" in color which served effectively as blinders when it came to exploring the richness of painting. The sophisticated awareness of art history distinguished Arthur Pope from other theorists. Pope isolated four major "modes of representation" in painting and noted that they evolved through time in Western art. Certain uses of color are inseparable from certain modes of representation, and as we consider these modes we shall see how they relate to aspects of color already considered.

The Linear Mode

The *mode of line and local color* is well described by its name, which can be shortened to *linear mode*. Lines define the forms of objects, which are further differentiated by their colors. These local colors may be like those in nature, as often with Chinese and Japanese painting; or fanciful, like some Rajput minia-

30
Paul Signac (1863-1935)
La Rochelle, 1922
Watercolor, 10¾ x 16⅞ inches
Gift of James N. Rosenberg, in memory
of Aaron and Nettie Naumburg,
1957.184

tures or paintings by Gauguin or Klee, for example. In either case there is usually a lack of concern with multiple planes of depth or qualities of solidity or light. Often an effect of one-plane or two-plane color dominates, and the organization is essentially that of a general uniformity of attraction reinforcing this effect. Such is the case in the Indian and Persian paintings in the exhibition (nos. 9-11).

The Sculptural Mode

In terms of growing complexity, as well as historical sequence within the European tradition, the next mode is concerned with the modeling of separate forms and can be called a *sculptural mode*. Pope referred to it as "mode of relief," since the separate forms in late Gothic and Renaissance Italian painting so often have more of a relief effect than a full round effect. This and subsequent modes belong only to European paintings; Asiatic painting did not develop much of a plastic sense until it was influenced by European art. Late Gothic Italian painting, like the painting by the Master of the Fogg Pietà (no. 31), grew out of earlier Gothic and Byzantine painting done in a linear mode, and the feeling of sharply differentiated local colors is retained. Even though Giotto's revolution has turned the figures into solid, space-occupying forms, these forms are close to the picture plane and the background slips snugly in behind them, preserving a good deal of the older two-dimensionalism in the color. In addition, each color field has its own kind of interest, and about the same degree of visual attraction—thus establishing the two-dimensionality of decorative color but now combined with a kind of counterpoint of modeled forms.

Characteristic of this sculptural mode is the absence of cast shadows. Since cast shadows are more a function of light than of sculptural form they were suppressed as long as this mode of painting dominated—in Italy for about two centuries, until the time of Leonardo da Vinci. Nor do the modeling shadows have any of the purpose of providing the illusion of light, such as found in Monet. Compared with the regularity with which the local colors in Monet's painting are modified by modeling (fig. 10) there seems to be no order in the Florentine painting (fig. 13). Instead, the order comes from weighing one kind of attraction against another: value contrast with the ground (left standing female figure); inherent intensity (Magdalen); internal value contrasts (rocks); and various combinations of these.

Ambrogio Lorenzetti's *Crucifixion* (no. 32) is even richer in the variety as well as the sensitivity of its color relations. Patterns and detailed passages enter in, as do even more varied types of modeling. Specific directions for painting in tempera with just the kinds of modeling used in these two paintings are to be found in the major source book of the period, Cennino Cennini's *Il Libro dell' Arte (The Craftsman's Handbook).*[4] The most recurrent method of model-

31

Master of the Fogg Pietà

Mourning Over the Body of Christ,
ca. 1325-1350

Tempera on panel, 16 x 19 inches

Gift of Paul J. Sachs, 1927.306

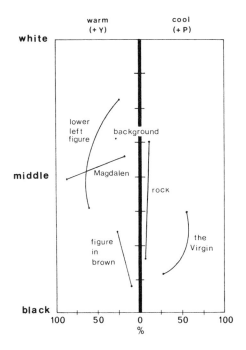

Figure 13
Value and intensity diagram of the Fogg
Pietà. *Compared with the systematic
modeling from light into shadow in
Monet's* Fish *(fig. 10) each color field in
this painting follows an independent
method of modeling. Some forms "up-
model," i.e., model from higher intensity
toward white (as in lower-left figure);
some "down-model," i.e., model from
higher intensity toward black (as in figure in brown); and some have a "hue-
shift" accompanying the modeling (as in
the Magdalen). Control is achieved by
generally equal color attraction.*

32
Ambrogio Lorenzetti (active 1323-1348)
Crucifixion, ca. 1337-1342
Tempera on panel, 24 x 11⅜ inches
Gift of Meta and Paul J. Sachs, 1939.113

ing is "up-modeling," or adding white to the basic pigment. This, too, has a decorative purpose because we tend to read shadowed areas as recessive surfaces, but if they are more intense than the lights they seek to come forward and reassert the plane of the surface. (See the figure in yellow to the right of the Virgin in the Pietà.) The result is an interesting tension between two- and three-dimensionalism.[5]

The Pictorial Mode

Another mode of representation which incorporates a different point of view toward color as well as a different attitude toward picture-making is the *pictorial mode,* often called the "Venetian mode" by Arthur Pope, because the Venetian painters of the sixteenth century brought it into being. Something very like it can be found in ancient Roman painting, in Baroque and Rococo work, and in artists like Cézanne who broke away from naturalism. The artist painting in a pictorial mode may or may not have a strong interest in plastic form (he usually has some); he may or may not have an interest in light effect, but he always is concerned with the broad pattern of lights and darks that make up his painting surface, and he uses color to achieve connections and disconnections across this surface and into the picture space. Rubens' *Wrath of Neptune* (no. 8) is an excellent example of pictorial painting. Passages of lights connect forms, as do passages of darks. Planes in space are created by arbitrarily lightening or darkening areas: note the light region just to the right of Neptune's body. In other regions the lights overlap the darks, resulting in a kind of interplay between light and dark throughout the picture. This arbitrary manipulation of tones was suggested to Rubens by Titian, whose works he had copied in Madrid a few years before he did this oil sketch.

Common characteristics run through the color in almost all of Baroque painting, whether naturalistic like Ruisdael's *Road Lined with Trees* (no. 27), or fanciful like Bazzani's *Feast in the House of Simon the Pharisee* (no. 33) and Tiepolo's *Apotheosis of Aeneas* (no. 46). What characterizes all of them is the interplay among three opposites: light-dark, warm-cool, and near-far. Since the light-dark contrasts are stronger than the warm-cool contrasts it is the former which generally provide the skeleton of the near-far, or spatial definition. They are available to the draftsman or printmaker as well. If we accept this definition of Baroque color we would have to recognize its continuation into the work of Turner, as in his *Simplon Pass* (no. 5). In fact, Turner in many ways prolonged a Baroque formal structure into the nineteenth century, in contrast to the other major landscapists of the period like Constable or Corot.

In this approach to painting the chief psychological or dramatic centers are usually marked by major contrasts. Unlike the Pietà, in which the attractions are

33

Giuseppe Bazzani (1701 [or 1690]-1769)
Feast in the House of Simon the Pharisee
Oil on canvas, 19½ x 53 inches
Gift of Jacob Heimann, 1944.16

nearly equal throughout, Rubens clearly emphasized Neptune and his horses through strong contrasts. Similarly in the Tiepolo we have no trouble focusing on the dramatic center of Aeneas and his symbol of Victory. Bazzani located his climax of contrasts at the table corner adjacent to the dramatic center of Mary Magdalen and the feet of Christ. Then the light-dark interchanges establish the spatial location of the figures in relation to the background and to each other. Hue shifts occur throughout the draperies, which are often enriched by under- and over-painting. Christ's under-robe is modeled in red and neutrals, then the upper robe is over-painted on this base with blue in the half-lights. The same blue is found in the Magdalen, but here it is down-modeled toward black. In addition to this complexity Bazzani put actual neutrals in the yellow-neutral setting so that they look cool (jug, armor, tablecloth).

Le Premier Pas de l'Enfance (no. 34) by Fragonard and Gérard seems almost literal in comparison with the painting by Bazzani. Yet one senses quite arbitrary warm-cool shifts in many passages, and the hues in the lower foreground move from left to right in a nice sequence of yellow-orange to an intense red-orange to a cool light red.

One would have to associate Cézanne's use of color with this pictorial approach to painting. In the *Auvers, Small Houses* (no. 35), an early painting by Cézanne, his characteristic color is just beginning to emerge, but there already is an interaction of warm and cool which constantly provides us with spatial cues. The interplay of warm and cool that we find in the houses (cool played into warm lights and warm played into cool shadows) suggests the treatment of color found in the other examples of this mode of representation.

34
Jean Honoré Fragonard (1732-1806) and
Marguerite Gérard (1761-1837)
Le Premier Pas de l'Enfance, ca. 1780
Oil on canvas, 17½ x 21¾ inches
Gift of Charles E. Dunlap, 1961.166

35
Paul Cézanne (1839-1906)
Auvers, Small Houses, ca. 1874-1875
Oil on canvas, 16 x 21½ inches
Bequest of Annie S. Coburn, 1934.28

36

Winslow Homer (1836-1910)

Homosassa Jungle in Florida, 1904

Watercolor, 14 x 22 inches

Gift of Mrs. Charles S. Homer, in
memory of the late Charles S. Homer and
his brother Winslow Homer, 1935.50

37
Winslow Homer (1836-1910)
The Trapper, Adirondacks, 1870
Oil on canvas, 19½ x 29½ inches
Colby College, Gift of Harold T.
Pulsifer Memorial

But a fine artist's use of color often eludes strict categorization. Winslow Homer's *Homosassa Jungle in Florida* (no. 36) is anchored more firmly in nature than many examples of pictorial painting. It captures the particular effect of setting sunlight, but the arbitrary accenting and suppression of color contrasts and of details in order to achieve clarity and readability are guided by thinking similar to that of Rubens. Dark and light are interchanged and many details are eliminated in the complex tangle of the jungle background.

The Visual Mode

The fourth mode of representation brings us back to one of the starting points of our discussion: the recording of light in painting. Pope called this the "mode of total visual effect," which, for general use, can be shortened to *visual mode.* This approach to representation is the only one which makes light its starting point, though the rendering of light is combined with other means of creating an illusion of reality such as perspective projection. Cast shadows are neither omitted nor suppressed, as they are with a sculptural approach to representation, nor are they willfully introduced for dramatic or decorative purposes, as in the Bazzani painting and other works done in a pictorial mode. Rather, cast shadows are more or less literally carried over from nature to further the illusion of light, and, as we noted with Monet's *Fish,* their hues consistently lower in value and intensity as less and less light enters them. Modeling shadows also darken and lose intensity as the surfaces of the forms turn away from the source of light.

Reflecting surfaces and variations in the color of the light provide further complications in the appearance of the local colors, but through all these changes one reads local colors into objects because of the phenomenon of *color constancy*. Once the identification of a local color with an object has been established we read that color into the object almost without regard to the changes it undergoes. In paintings executed in a visual mode this interaction between light, shadow, reflections, colored lights, and color constancy often becomes a dominant theme.

Consider the painting by Charles Sheeler, *Upper Deck* (no. 38), as a set of special problems in light effect, including the problem of the adaptation of the eye to differing illuminations. Our eyes, like the artist's when he was studying the real subject, are adapted to the high luminosity of sunlit whites. The interiors of the ventilation pipes, therefore, are recorded as black. The local colors are mostly neutrals to begin with, so that color variations are due to other factors, chiefly the different colors of light sources. The dominant source is the sun, which is essentially white light. The sky colors many shadow areas with its blue light, and the reflected light from the deck tinges other shadow areas with yellow. In addition Sheeler pushes the effects of simultaneous contrast by darkening the shadows when they approach either the sky or the sunlit whites and cooling the edges of the cast shadows on the warm deck.

Another way in which local colors are modified in nature, and in painting done in a visual mode, is through their recession into the distance. The resulting effect of atmospheric perspective is due to a regular reduction of contrasts in value and intensity. Winslow Homer's *The Trapper, Adirondacks* (no. 37) illustrates how, as the intervening layer of atmosphere becomes thicker, the local colors are pulled toward the atmospheric tone. This effect is accompanied by a blueing of colors with increasing distance. The reason for this is the same reason the sky is blue: atmospheric particles interfere with light waves, but they do so selectively: the shorter (blue) wavelengths are deflected more than the longer (red) ones. The diffusion of blue particles has an increasing effect on the distant colors, especially the darks, as is particularly evident in the lightening and cooling of the warm darks as we move from the nearer island to the next island and to the land beyond. The mountainside at the far left has become almost completely absorbed by the atmospheric tone. But the light local colors are able to penetrate the atmosphere and, because light from them has lost some short wavelengths through diffusion, appear as warm. The warmth is especially seen in the light parts of the clouds, though Homer introduces a few warm flecks of light in the distant forest as well. The low sun itself has a warm light, as can be seen in its reflections off the log.

Childe Hassam also registers an atmospheric effect in his *Headlands* (no. 39). With the depth of space much less, the local colors in the further rocks are pulled toward a light neutral instead of a blue by the atmospheric tone. Whether the

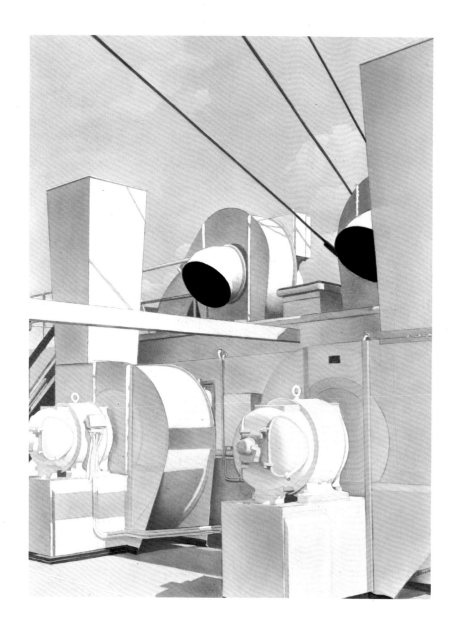

38

Charles Sheeler (1883-1965)

Upper Deck, 1929

Oil on canvas, 29⅛ x 22⅛ inches

Purchase: Louise E. Bettens Fund, 1933.97

39
Childe Hassam (1859-1935)
Headlands, 1908
Oil on canvas, 24¼ x 29¼ inches
Gift of Archer M. Huntington,
1936.131

40
Claude Monet (1840-1926)
La Cabane du Douanier, 1897
Oil on canvas, 25½ x 36 inches (sight)
Gift of Ella Milbank Foshay, 1972.31

reduction in the intensity of the warm colors in the further plane can be attributed more to the neutralizing effect of atmosphere or to the artist's use of color for the illusion of space, as discussed earlier, is a question that we probably do not need to decide. The two are not identical, inasmuch as the control of contrasts for conveying space is an artistic device while the regular reduction of contrasts in the atmosphere is a natural phenomenon. But in painting in the visual mode they approach being identical.

Childe Hassam's painting, with its broken touches of color, is an example of Impressionism, a late development in the history of painting in the visual mode. A generation earlier Monet and others had begun exaggerating intensities to the point where they threatened to break out of a relation with the value scale of painting. In order to prevent this, these first Impressionists applied their intense colors in separate strokes so that they would partially neutralize each other through additive, or optical, mixing. In addition they gained the effect characterized by Pissarro as "stirring up luminosities more intense than those created by mixed pigments."[6] Childe Hassam's painting illustrates both these qualities of broken color. The rocks in nature were close to gray, an effect the artist secured by juxtaposing a warm brown and a cool blue. In addition, the effect of light is enhanced by the lively play of these two hues. Value constancy within an area is a requisite for effective Impressionist color mixing as can be noticed here in the closeness of values of the brown and blue within any one region of the rocks.

Another painting by Claude Monet illustrates the extraordinary balance between representational color and color organized within the painting itself that was often achieved in Impressionism. In the *La Cabane du Douanier* (no. 40), most of the land mass is painted with two hues, a red and a green. Closer inspection reveals yellows brought into the light mass on the right and blues into the central shadow areas. Red (as pink) emerges most strongly in the lighted edges of the rocky hills, and green is dominant in many of the half-lights. Blue is limited to the darker shadows where also a few purples result from a mixture of the earthy red and the blue. But nothing in the painting is very dark; the whole being brought into a luminous range of about middle value to white. This differs from the "crowded lights" effect seen in Turner's *Simplon Pass* (no. 5) where the lights were contrasted with a few accents of strong dark.

THE SIMULTANEOUS FUNCTIONS OF COLOR IN ART

The painting by Monet points up a basic fact about color in painting—especially successful color in painting—namely, that it seldom accomplishes only one thing. Rather it presents us simultaneously with a believable parallel to nature's

41
Frans Hals (1580-1666)
Portrait of a Preacher, ca. 1625
Oil on canvas, 24 x 20 inches
Naumburg Bequest, 1930.186

color and with a coherent internal color organization belonging to the artifact itself. Our last series of paintings has been chosen to make this point in relation to a single problem—that of painting a portrait head.

The significant point about the modeling of heads in our three examples is that there are orderly changes in the hues and intensities of colors in the flesh which accompany the changes in value in the modeling. Frans Hals' *Portrait of a Preacher* (no. 41) presents it very simply because much of the modeling here is done in yellowish neutral (nearly monochrome); into this are then introduced touches of red that fit perfectly into the value gradations, while adding the warmth of flesh color. J. S. Copley's *Colonels Hugo and Schleppergrell* (no. 42) is more complex, with a red, yellow, neutral range of hues intermixed again with gradations of value so that hue and intensity gradations interplay with them. A few touches reveal the red tone (perhaps a Venetian red with some vermilion added) as it was laid out on the palette; the yellow (a yellow ochre most likely) and the neutral (already pre-mixed with some yellow to keep it from looking too blue) also as they were laid out on the palette. We know a good deal about

42

John Singleton Copley (1738-1815)

Portrait of Colonels Hugo and Schleppergrell, 1787

Oil on canvas, 26 x 22 inches

Gift of Mrs. Gordon Dexter, 1942.180

palette arrangements in the seventeenth and eighteenth centuries because of notes by painters and because working palettes were often included in self-portraits or portraits of other artists. The appearance of Copley's palette, if we could see it, would most likely indicate the kind of orderly gradations we see in the paintings themselves.

The central head in Renoir's *At the Milliner's* (no. 43) is similar in its color gradations to the Hals and Copley except that the more sprightly touch of Impressionism has come in along with more striking color contrasts. All of the Impressionists and Post-impressionists sought models for the kind of order they desired in paintings of the sixteenth through the eighteenth centuries. Curiously, the Academy, which was supposed to preserve tradition, had let some of these fundamentals of tradition slip away and the progressive artists had to rediscover them for themselves.

In some ways what we are seeing in these three portraits is a very close relation between drawing and painting—drawing with color, it could be called. The strokes of the brush are rightly placed to define the form and at the same time selected to keep the color organization going. Deciding on the stroke to use and the color to mix are not separate acts but both part of the same act. This is the essence of what Cézanne hammered out from his study of the Old Masters.

Less obvious is the fusion of brush stroke and choice of color in the still life *Woodcock and Quail* by J. B. Oudry (no. 44). But it is no less significant as the subtle changes of warm to cool accompany equal subtle sequences of brush strokes that define the natural order of the forms and their feathers. Sensitive color variations within the strictly limited palette make the color range seem greater. The additional factor of thin to thicker paint also relates to the bringing forward or placing back of forms in space.

This painting brings out one last point that should be made about color in painting in this brief survey—the artist's responsiveness to the pigments and the medium he uses. Essentially, this has to do with thinness or thickness (impasto) of paint, and the opacity or transparency of the pigment. Oudry exploits the transparency of his warm pigment (probably burnt sienna) and the opacity of his white. The difference is felt between a glaze (transparent paint drawn thinly over a surface) and a scumble (opaque paint, also drawn thinly over, but not quite covering the usually darker tone beneath). All the artists in this discussion have been sensitive to these characteristics of paint and pigment. The Master of the Pietà responded to the transparency of the madder reds in the figure on the extreme right; Rubens ran a gamut from transparent thinness to opaque impasto in both the horses' heads. In short there is more to understanding color quality in painting than can be explained with hue, value, and intensity. But it is equally certain that these are the basic qualities of color.

43
Pierre Auguste Renoir (1841-1919)
At the Milliner's, ca. 1876
Oil on canvas, 12¾ x 9⅝ inches
Bequest of Annie S. Coburn, 1934.31

44
Jean Baptiste Oudry (1686-1755)
Woodcock and Quail, 1749
Oil on canvas, 25 x 18¾ inches
Purchase: Alpheus Hyatt Fund, 1945.16

Two paintings from the Fogg's collection have been selected to summarize our treatment of color, Renoir's *Spring Bouquet* (no. 45) and Tiepolo's *Apotheosis of Aeneas* (no. 46). Both reveal a superb sense of decorative color, Renoir in a visual mode of representation and Tiepolo in a pictorial mode. Renoir distributed his masses of white and light pinks across the canvas, scattering yellows, blue-purples, and greens between. Fundamentally everything is obedient to a single light source and the general paleness adds to the luminosity. Again the fact that color is paint makes itself felt, but not through differences of transparency and opacity since all the paint is opaque. Rather it is the slightly amorphous brush stroke that transforms the multiple textures inherent in the subject (petals, leaves, porcelain, and stucco) into a new unity of paint and color.

Tiepolo's oil study for the ceiling fresco in the anteroom of the throne room of the Royal Palace in Madrid depicts the ascent of Aeneas to the realm of his mother, Venus. At the same time that we sense an overall coherence of the decorative color we are strongly aware of the illusion of space going up and back, marked off by three major planes and several intermediate ones. How Tiepolo manages to maintain both these effects is worth studying. The lower terrestrial plane, with armorers fashioning Aeneas's arms below, is terminated by the figure of Time with whom Aeneas has left his armor. This general plane is where the strongest contrasts are located. White is opposed to black, and red and blue appear in fairly high intensities. The light-to-shadow contrasts are strongest and characterized by neutralized shadows, especially in the foreground reclining figure and the upper part of Time's figure.

The second plane, with Aeneas and his companions Victory and Fame, has the same hues of red and blue as below but less intense as they move toward white. Further, they are stronger in the half-lights or shadows rather than in the lights, as below. Aeneas's large red area is somewhat absorbed by the warm cloud behind, while Victory's blue robe goes into a warm neutral shadow in order not to contrast too strongly with the white cloud behind, but strong enough to give some accent near the painting's center. In fact most of the strong value contrasts in the whole painting are between the neutralish colors while the strongest intensities are placed in a setting of values close to themselves. This equalizing of hue and intensity contrasts with value contrasts is highly characteristic of decorative color.

The third major plane with Venus and her companions has many fewer darks and the only intensity that is allowed to sing out is that of the yellow robe, again in a setting that minimizes the value contrasts. The most intense flesh colors are now in the shadows; if we compare the colorful shadows in the far right figure on the cloud with the neutral shadows of the bottom reclining male figure, the difference is striking. This is not simply atmospheric perspective, as the further

45
Pierre Auguste Renoir (1841-1919)
Spring Bouquet, 1866
Oil on canvas, 40⅝ x 31 inches
Bequest of Grenville L. Winthrop,
1943.277

46
Giovanni Domenico Tiepolo (1727-1804)
Apotheosis of Aeneas, ca. 1766
Oil on canvas, 28⁷⁄₁₆ x 20⅛ inches
Purchase: Allston Burr Bequest Fund,
1949.76

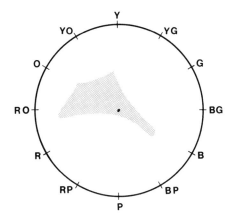

Figure 14
Hue and intensity diagram of Tiepolo's Apotheosis of Aeneas. *The color range is wider here than in Rubens'* Wrath of Neptune. *But still there are many hues that are either absent or very reduced in intensity, particularly the purples and the greens.*

shadow is not approaching an atmospheric tone, but, rather, a different scheme of modeling for different planes in space. In addition it brings out the expressive difference between the earth-bound male figures and the celestial character of the Venus-group. Symbolic of the difference is the pale gold, white-plumed helmet that Venus will present to her son in contrast with the grey-black armor he has left behind.

The last figure in our zig-zag path upward is Mercury who returns us to a nearer plane again. The kinship of his red helmet with Aeneas's red robe and his flesh tones to those of Aeneas helps to locate him in a similar spatial plane. The upward-backward movement has been halted.

The hue and intensity range in the total painting is keyed to a red (slightly orange), a warm yellow, and a blue, plus black and white. Though the range seems full it is restricted to the shaded area in figure 14. The greens are extremely neutral, oranges are only those that result from the red-yellow mixture, and all purples are entirely omitted. There is a recurrent warm color, orange in hue, that belongs to the toning of the ground. It is allowed to show in many flesh areas and in the clouds and Venus's chariot in the upper right. It also shows through the blue sky, the paint being applied so as not to cover completely. If any particular hue acts as a unifier, it is this warm orange.

The important movement up and down the surface is kept going partly by the warm-cool interplay mentioned earlier as associated with Baroque-Rococo art. The very foreground is warm, followed by the cool white rock on which Time sits; then comes a warm cloud, followed by a cool white cloud atop of which sits Venus. We return to warm at the right side and behind Venus and Aeneas, with cool sky finishing this large alternation from bottom to top. Within these larger planes are many minor warm-cool passages; one is enough to focus upon: the richly spatial lower side of Aeneas's cloud which, although dominantly warm, passes imperceptibly into cool neutrals. And of the three winged *putti* the first is warm, the second and third cooler, and then there is a return to warm in the third *putto's* leg and foot as the cloud behind it turns cool.

There are other methods of approaching color in art than those that have been sketched in here. The realm of symbolism, touched on briefly in reference to the helmet of Venus, is otherwise absent. Examination of such symbolism could obviously be carried further but, given direction by Arthur Pope's approach, the emphasis has been on color organization, or color as an aspect of artistic form. Cézanne is supposed to have spoken of "the logic of color." Perhaps that is what we are dealing with; but this quotation goes on: "the painter owes obedience to this [logic of color] alone, never to the logic of the mind. If he surrenders to the latter he is lost."[7] This thought should also be present in our minds as we explain color relationships with the aid of a conceptual model of the color world.

The Pope Color Solid

This supplement starts with a revision of the basic description of the color solid written by Arthur Pope sometime before 1920 and revised on three different occasions to serve as a part of the first chapter of the several editions of his book on the language of drawing and painting.* The last revision completed by Pope himself appeared in *The Language of Drawing and Painting* (1949).

The changes by Howard Fisher, designed to make the description as useful as possible to modern readers, followed extensive correspondence and meetings with Pope. Those interested in the precise nature of the adjustments made, or in the historical development of Pope's color concepts in relation to creative work in the arts, should consult the full original texts as well as his other writings. The general nature of the changes made for this supplement can be highlighted as follows:

1. Minor adjustments were made to achieve more ready comprehension, such as separating the color solid at yellow rather than red, and repeating yellow left and right.

2. Certain portions of the original material, both text and illustrations, which were not considered significant for present purposes have been omitted—such as Pope's discussion of the concept of *neutralization.*

3. The terminology used by Pope was unusual in several respects, and it has been modified for greater clarity, or in some cases to conform with modern usage. Examples are the use of percentages rather than common fractions in defining relative intensity, or the use of the word *color* rather than *tone* for color in general, including neutrals.

4. A few adjustments have been made to reflect research by color scientists since the period of Pope's most active work—such as giving recognition to the now generally accepted belief that visually equal spacing is impossible to achieve within a color solid.

5. Emphasis has been placed throughout on the appearance of color, rather than on methods for its production, and references to specific pigments have been omitted.

6. Pope, as well as Denman Ross, failed to appreciate the importance of the concept of relative intensity, which they used, in contrast to the concept of "chroma" developed by A. H. Munsell. The original text was not well-defined in this connection, and it has been adjusted to clarify and stress this feature of the Pope solid.

7. Several new diagrams have been added, and the original diagrams have been redrawn with some modifications. (Additional diagrams and commentary follow the revision of Pope's text.)

*See the bibliography at the end of this volume for a complete listing of Pope's writings. The preface to Pope's *Tone Relations in Painting* is dated January 1922. In it, Pope refers to "This pamphlet, a large portion of which in typewritten form has been in use for several years ...."

The Form of the Color Solid

Arthur Pope

With revisions, additional diagrams, and commentary by Howard T. Fisher

FACTORS IN COLOR

When we say that we see objects existing in space, what actually happens is that they are projected upon the retina of the eye by rays of light traveling from the objects to the eye. This projection on the retina of the eye is a two-dimensional image (the visual image) and corresponds to a cross-section of the cone of light converging on the eye. It is like the image formed on the ground-glass plate of a camera.

The visual image is composed of areas distinguished from one another by differences in quantity and quality of light. These areas may be placed high or low, to the right or to the left in the field of vision in relation to its center; they may be large or small in relation to other areas; they may be round, or square, or oval, or some other shape—that is, they may vary in *position, size,* and *shape.* These areas may also be light or dark; they may be red or yellow or green or blue, or some intermediate hue, or they may be neutral gray; they may be strong in red or yellow or some other hue, or they may be weak in hue—grayish.

In other words, if we use the term *darkness* (or "value") to indicate the relative degree of lightness or darkness, the term *hue* to indicate the variable quality due to varying combinations of the wavelengths which make up white light, and the term *intensity* to indicate the strength of the hue as distinguished from neutrality, we may say that these areas vary in *darkness, hue,* and *intensity.* We may also say that the visual image is made up of areas varying in *color* (that is, in darkness, hue, and intensity) and arranged in different positions, sizes, and shapes. We may define the visual image by defining the position, the size, the shape, and the color of each of its areas. We define the color of an area by defining its darkness, its hue, and its intensity; or in the case of a neutral color (white or black or an intermediate gray), which is at the zero point of intensity and hence has no hue, by defining its darkness. While colors possessing hue are distinguished from each other by differences of darkness, hue, and intensity, neutral tones are distinguished by differences of darkness only.

With pigment materials spread on a flat surface such as paper or canvas, we may produce areas which, like those composing the visual image, have extension in two dimensions. We may make these areas light or dark; we may make them red or yellow, or some other hue; and we may make them strong in that hue, or weak, or neutral gray. We may give these areas different positions, different sizes, and different shapes. Thus, the terms of art and graphic design are like the terms of vision—*colors* produced by pigment materials, varying in *darkness* (or "value"), *hue,* and *intensity,* and arranged in different *positions, sizes,* and *shapes.*

Other words are often used in place of these, and the same words are frequently used in other meanings, often very vaguely. It must be borne in mind that it does not much matter what terms we use, so long as we define them clearly and use them consistently to express the different factors involved. Numerous other terms are regularly used in color work but they frequently have meanings (or alternative meanings) that range from the highly specialized to the worth-

white 1

high light 2

light 3

low light 4

middle 5

high dark 6

dark 7

low dark 8

black 9

Figure 15
The scale of darkness, showing the 9 darkness levels and 8 darkness steps.

lessly vague. Consequently, except when specifically defined or employed in certain special contexts, their use can frequently lead to confusion.[1]

COLOR SCALES

In order to think and talk definitely about color and color relations, we must establish definite classifications or scales by which we may differentiate among the factors or elements in any color. So, leaving aside for the present the question of positions, sizes, and shapes, let us consider possibilities for the classification and scaling of colors with regard to darkness (or "value"), hue, and intensity —and the expression of the relations of these factors by graphic diagrams. All such classifications are necessarily subjective in nature, and an infinite number might be made, but the following scale concepts published by Denman W. Ross are particularly useful for our purposes.[2]

For the present, we may confine our attention to the scales and the diagrams based upon them, in order to obtain a good understanding of the opportunities which they afford for clearer thought regarding color. The diagrams, which express graphically the relations of hue, darkness, and intensity will be found of much assistance in achieving a clear understanding of the principles governing color relations both in nature and in art, and especially useful in considering design in terms of color relations.

The Scale of Darkness

A convenient scale of darkness in neutral tones (that is, colors without hue or intensity) may be arranged as shown in figure 15. With white and black as start-

ing points, other darkness levels may then be located as shown, the words *high* and *low* referring to relative position in the diagram. This gives a convenient scale of nine darknesses (and eight darkness steps) with roughly equal visual spacing. Since the terms used are slightly cumbersome, for easy reference the various darkness levels (starting with *white*) will be identified by the numbers 1 through 9. Thus, for example, the number 5 will correspond to *middle darkness,* while the number 9 will correspond to *black.*

This scale of nine darknesses gives sufficiently small intervals for ordinary purposes and can be easily visualized with a fair degree of accuracy. The darknesses are relative rather than absolute; that is, they are relative to white and black as commonly encountered, in contrast to theoretically perfect white and black.*

The Scale of Hue

A convenient scale of hue, at the highest intensity commonly encountered, may be arranged as shown in figure 16. Red, yellow, and blue are placed at equal intervals in a circular scheme. With these as starting points, the other hues may then be located. This gives a convenient scale of twelve hues (and twelve hue steps) with roughly equal visual spacing. In the center of the circle, we may place gray (including white and black as the extremes of gray), which we designate neutral. This scale of twelve hues gives sufficiently small intervals for ordinary purposes and can be easily visualized

*For a discussion of the problem of darkness scaling, see this Supplement, pp. 115-117.

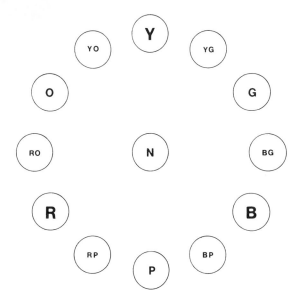

Figure 16
The scale of hue, showing the 12 hues of the color circle, with neutral in the center.

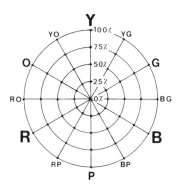

Figure 17
The scale of intensity, showing the 12 hues and the 5 relative intensities.

with a fair degree of accuracy.*

For convenience, the hues between yellow and purple on the left side of the hue circle may be spoken of in a general way as the *warm hues*, and those between yellow and purple on the right side as the *cool hues*.

It will be noted that the different hues at high intensity tend to occur at different darknesses, with a marked overall tendency toward increasing darkness as the hues progress around either side of the hue circle from yellow to purple. If the hues are compared with the darkness scale, it will be found that Y corresponds in darkness approximately to *high light* (level 2), that YO and YG come approximately at *light* (level 3), O and G at *low light* (level 4), RO and BG at *middle darkness* (level 5), R and B at *high dark* (level 6), RP and BP at *dark* (level 7), and P at *low dark* (level 8).

THE SCALE OF INTENSITY

A convenient scale of intensity for each hue may be arranged as in figure 17. With neutral (0%) and high intensity (100%) as starting points, other intensity levels may then be located as shown. This gives a convenient scale of five intensities (and four intensity steps) with roughly equal visual spacing.

This scale of five intensities gives sufficiently small intervals for ordinary purposes and can be easily visualized with a fair degree of accuracy. The intensities are relative to the highest intensity commonly encountered for each hue.†

---

*For a discussion of the problem of hue scaling, see this Supplement, pp. 117-118.

†For a discussion of the problem of intensity scaling, see this Supplement, pp. 118-120.

TWO-DIMENSIONAL REPRESENTATIONS OF DARKNESS AND INTENSITY

For each of the twelve hues, the darkness and intensity possibilities may be represented as follows, using red-orange as an example.

Let the vertical line in figure 18 represent the scale of neutral grays from white to black inclusive, and also 0% intensity. Red-orange of high or 100% intensity comes approximately at the level of middle darkness, but it is distinguished from the neutral of middle darkness by its red-orange hue and by its intensity of 100%. In making the diagram we may then place RO of 100% intensity at the level of middle darkness, and at a convenient distance laterally (to represent 100%).

In relation to white and black and the neutrals between them, this position may serve to represent with sufficient accuracy for our purposes the darkness and the intensity of RO at high intensity.

If we wish to lighten 100% RO, to some level above middle darkness, we must introduce the element of white (or of some other neutral above middle darkness). But when we introduce the element of white we move toward white (which has an intensity of 0%) approximately along the line between 100% RO and white, reducing intensity as we go. If we wish to darken 100% RO we must introduce the element of black (or of some other neutral below middle darkness). But when we introduce the element of black we move toward black (which has an intensity of 0%) approximately along the line between 100% RO and black, reducing intensity as we go.

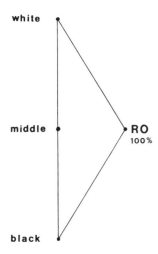

Figure 18
The darkness and intensity possibilities of red-orange—a constant-hue triangle with the vertical line representing neutral, or 0% intensity.

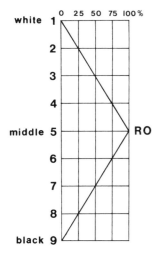

Figure 19
The darkness and intensity possibilities of red-orange with scale lines added— as in figure 18, but with horizontal lines of uniform darkness and vertical lines of uniform intensity.

Thus, if we move either up or down from the starting point (at 100% intensity) we reduce the intensity of the hue. Hence, the triangle shown in figure 18 expresses approximately all the possible combinations of darkness and intensity applicable to red-orange. We may have the hue quality of red-orange at any of the darknesses and intensities within the limits of the triangle.

Within the RO triangle of figure 19 each of the vertical lines shows approximate uniformity in terms of relative intensity, while each of the horizontal lines shows approximate uniformity in terms of darkness.

For each of the other eleven hues of the hue scale we may make similar triangles with such lines of uniformity, as shown in figure 20. (See also color chart 2.) Since the scale is for relative intensity, that is, intensity relative to high or 100% intensity for each hue, the triangles are all made the same width.[3]

Note that in figure 20 (and later in other figures) the hue circle has been separated at yellow, the lightest of the hues at 100% intensity, and that yellow has been repeated left and right in order for us to be able to illustrate all successive hue relationships.

THREE-DIMENSIONAL REPRESENTATIONS OF THE COLOR SOLID

A three-dimensional diagram, expressing simultaneously relations of darkness (or "value"), hue, and intensity, can be made by taking the triangles of the twelve hues and placing them together so that their neutral lines coincide. Neutral thus forms a vertical axis from which the 12 constant-hue triangles ra-

diate outward in the sequence of the hue circle. A view looking straight toward the warm side of such a three-dimensional diagram or color solid appears in figure 21. (Other views looking slightly down from above are shown in figures 25-29.)

If the solid is thought of as being enclosed in an imaginary cylinder representing 100% intensity, the 12 hues at their highest intensities will all touch the cylinder. Hues of less than 100% intensity will not touch the cylinder.

The color solid, thus constructed on the basis of the 12 constant-hue triangles, is symmetrical in three ways: (1) about a vertical plane passing through Y, N, and P; (2) inversely, about a vertical plane passing through RO, N, and BG; and (3) inversely, about a horizontal plane passing through middle darkness (level 5).

The vertical line from white to black forms the neutral axis of the solid. As we move around the neutral axis we get changes of hue; as we move up or down, we get changes of darkness; as we move outward or inward, we get changes of intensity. On any vertical *plane* radiating from the neutral axis, there is approximate uniformity of hue (while darkness and intensity vary); on any horizontal *plane* there is approximate uniformity of darkness (while hue and intensity vary); on any vertical *cylindrical* section centered on the neutral axis, there is approximate uniformity of intensity (while darkness and hue vary).

Figure 22 shows a chart of the 12 hues at their highest relative intensities for each of the nine darknesses (or "values") between white and black inclusive. This represents all the main colors on the

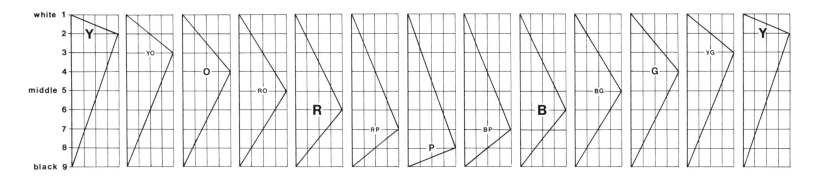

Figure 20
The darkness and intensity possibilities
of the 12 hues, with scale lines shown—
the 12 constant-hue triangles, with that
for Y repeated.

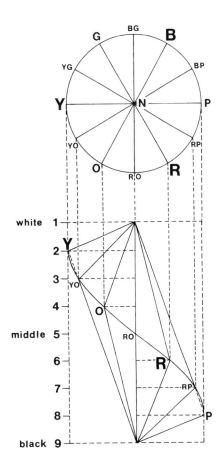

Figure 21
The color solid, based on the 12 con-
stant-hue triangles. Above, *looking*
down on the top at the color circle of
100% intensity; below, *looking toward*
the warm side.

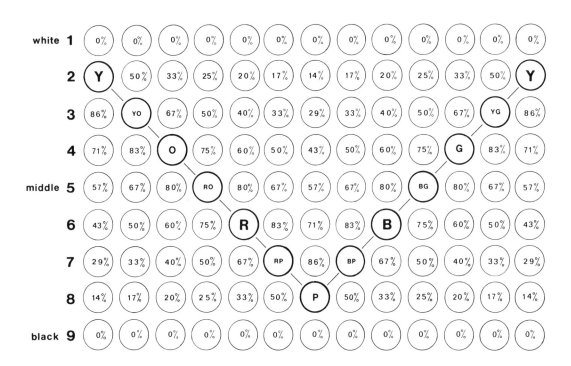

white 1	0%	0%	0%	0%	0%	0%	0%	0%	0%	0%	0%	0%	0%
2	**Y**	50%	33%	25%	20%	17%	14%	17%	20%	25%	33%	50%	**Y**
3	86%	YO	67%	50%	40%	33%	29%	33%	40%	50%	67%	YG	86%
4	71%	83%	**O**	75%	60%	50%	43%	50%	60%	75%	**G**	83%	71%
middle 5	57%	67%	80%	RO	80%	67%	57%	67%	80%	BG	80%	67%	57%
6	43%	50%	60%	75%	**R**	83%	71%	83%	**B**	75%	60%	50%	43%
7	29%	33%	40%	50%	67%	RP	86%	BP	67%	50%	40%	33%	29%
8	14%	17%	20%	25%	33%	50%	**P**	50%	33%	25%	20%	17%	14%
black 9	0%	0%	0%	0%	0%	0%	0%	0%	0%	0%	0%	0%	0%

Figure 22
The outer surface of the color solid, as if projected outward onto the enclosing cylinder, and then separated at Y and flattened. The points of 100% intensity fall along the diagonals indicated by the dashed line and hue letters, with relative intensity at other points as indicated.

Figure 23
Horizontal constant-darkness (or "constant-value") slices through the color solid at the 7 intermediate darknesses, with the outer dashed circles representing 100% intensity and the lesser intensity circles omitted.

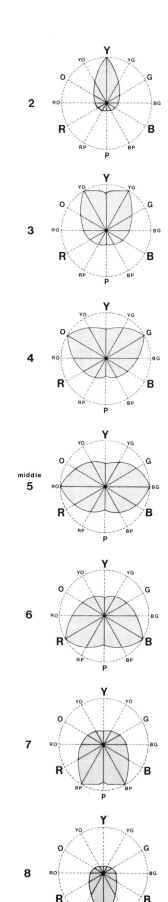

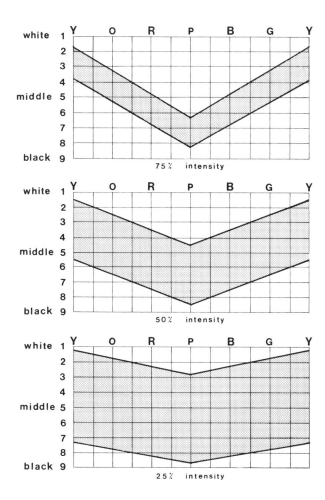

Figure 24
Vertical constant-intensity cylindrical slices through the color solid—separated at Y and stretched out flat to a uniform width (at the 3 intermediate intensities).

outside surface of the color solid, as if projected outward onto the enclosing cylinder and then separated at yellow and flattened. The colors shown by hue letters are of 100% intensity; all of the others are relative to these and of lesser intensity as indicated by the figures. Colors in vertical columns are all of approximately the same hue, while colors in horizontal rows are all of approximately the same darkness. Intensity varies from 0% (for white and black) to 100% for the 12 hues at high intensity.

To express relations of darkness, hue, and intensity *all at the same time,* or to represent approximate contrasts among colors generally, it is necessary to use the three-dimensional diagram of the color solid. However, two-dimensional diagrams may be used to express all possible relations between any two factors without regard to the third. When so used, care must be taken to avoid possible misunderstanding, as this type of two-factor chart can be dangerously misleading if the third factor varies to any significant degree.

We have already considered two-dimensional representations of darkness and intensity as shown by vertical radial slices in terms of the constant-hue triangles.

TWO-DIMENSIONAL REPRESENTATIONS OF HUE AND INTENSITY

Horizontal constant-darkness (or "constant value") slices through the color solid for each of seven darknesses are shown in figure 23 (and also in figure 26). These clearly illustrate the possibilities of hue and intensity at the seven intermediate levels of darkness, namely levels

2 through 8. At darkness levels 1 and 9 the solid comes to a point, and hence only white and black respectively would appear. Once again, as within the constant-hue slices, the straight-line distance between any two points conforms at least roughly to the magnitude of the visual contrast between the colors represented by such points—in this case in terms of hue and intensity of the same darkness.

At approximately *high light* (level 2), Y comes at highest intensity (100%), while other hues can be obtained only at considerably less intensity—with the purple region obtainable only at very low intensity.

At approximately *light* (level 3), YO and YG reach highest intensity (100%), while Y moves in toward the neutral axis. The other hues become a little more intense as they move out from the neutral axis.

At approximately *low light* (level 4), the situation is somewhat similar but with O and G at highest intensity. At *middle darkness* (level 5), we get a symmetrical pattern. RO and BG are at highest intensity, while purples and yellows are of intermediate intensity.

The patterns then repeat in reverse. For example, at *low dark* (level 8) in contrast to *high light* (level 2), it is P which comes at highest intensity (100%), while other hues can be obtained only at considerably less intensity—with the yellow region obtainable only at very low intensity.

Light red is called pink in ordinary speech, while the yellows and oranges in the lower darknesses are vaguely called tans and browns. But at most only the *names* are affected by changes of

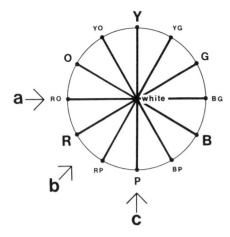

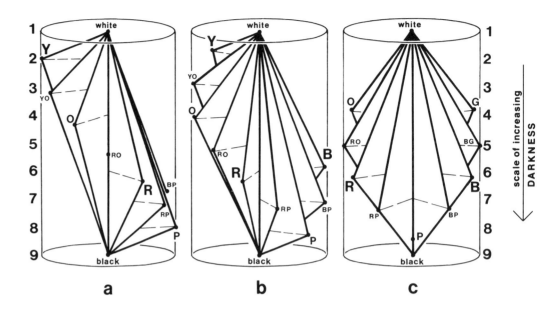

Figure 25

Vertical radial slices are shown through the solid, each slice corresponding to one of the 12 basic hue positions. The high-intensity (100%) line passes through the dots with accompanying hue abbreviations. The line would show on the surface of the enclosing cylinder, but for simplicity it has here been omitted from the oblique views.

darkness. Every possible hue, of course, can be obtained at every possible darkness (or "value") between white and black.*

TWO-DIMENSIONAL REPRESENTATIONS OF HUE AND DARKNESS

Vertical constant-intensity cylindrical slices through the color solid for each of three intensities clearly illustrate the possibilities of hue and darkness for the three intermediate intensities of 25%, 50%, and 75%. At intensity 0%, only neutrals would appear; at intensity 100%, only the high intensities would appear. If separated at yellow and stretched out, such slices would appear as shown in figure 24. (See figure 27 for such slices in their original cylindrical form and see color chart 4, p. 26).

*See also color chart 3, p. 22.

ADDITIONAL DIAGRAMS AND COMMENTARY BY HOWARD T. FISHER

Oblique Views of the Color Solid

To help the reader visualize the three-dimensional relationships of the Pope color solid and understand the nature of the principal slices that may be made through it, several drawings have been prepared as seen from an angle (figs. 25-29). Each includes a plan view as seen from directly above, and three oblique views as seen from different angles identified on the plan. Studied in combination these oblique views make clear the nature of the Pope geometric concept.

Sampling Locations

There are 175 standard sampling locations for the Pope solid. Of these, nine are neutrals or what we may call *achromatic*—one at white, one at black, and seven at intermediate darkness locations.

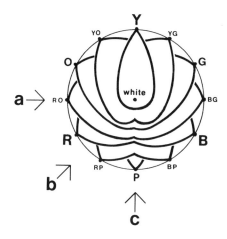

Figure 26
Horizontal slices are shown through the solid, each slice corresponding to one of the 7 intermediate darkness positions. At darkness levels 1 and 9 (not slices) only white and black respectively are present. On the oblique views, high-intensity is shown by the dashed line.

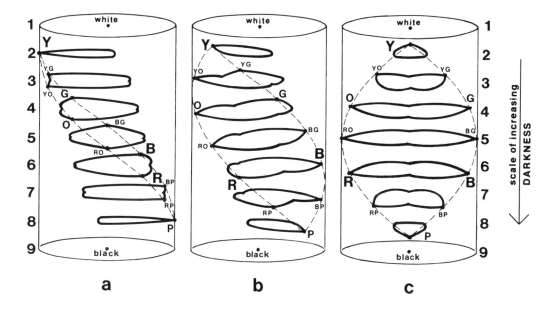

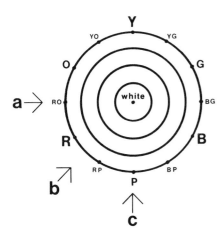

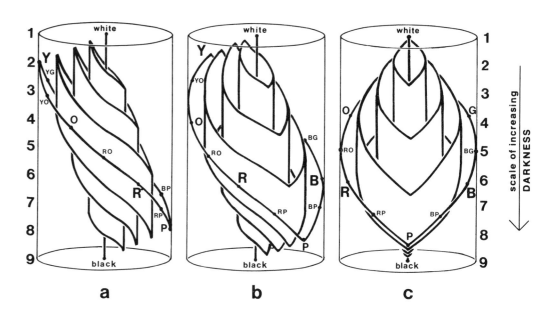

Figure 27
Vertical cylindrical slices are shown through the solid, each slice corresponding to one of the three intermediate intensity positions (25%, 50%, and 75% respectively, starting with the slice nearest the center). At 100% intensity (not a slice) only high intensities are present; at 0% intensity (not a slice) only neutrals are present.

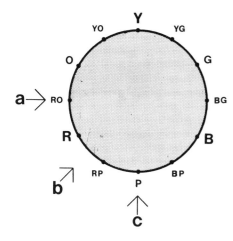

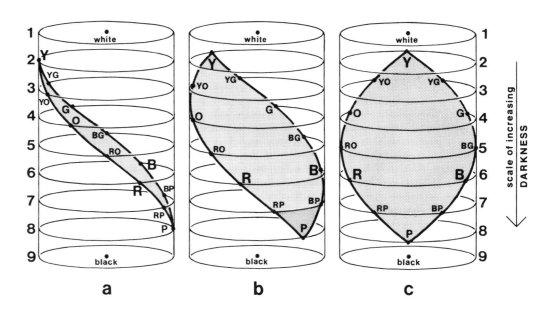

Figure 28
The traditional color circle, adjusted to conform to the darknesses or ("values") at 100% intensity. Yellow is light and purple dark, with a steady progression of increasing darkness when moving downward from Y to P.

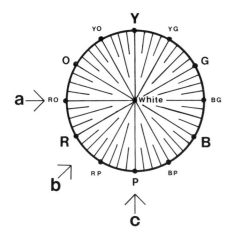

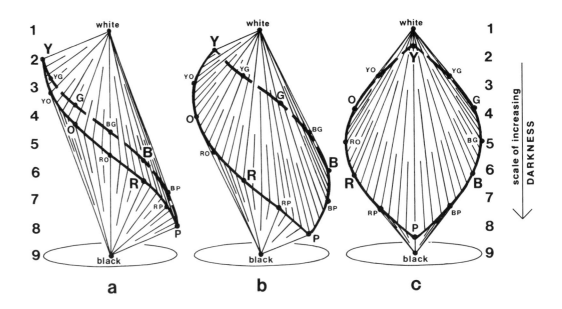

Figure 29
The exterior form of the color solid, as if formed by an infinite number of constant-hue triangles. Only 48 hues are actually represented by lines, in terms of two successive re-subdivisions of the basic 12-hue color circle. In this diagram the enclosing cylinder has been omitted for simplicity, and to stress the shape of the solid itself.

The remaining 166 are *chromatic*—that is, characterized by both hue and intensity.

The locations of the 166 chromatic sampling points may be shown in three different ways:

1. In terms of constant-hue vertical slices (fig. 30 and color chart 2).
2. In terms of constant-darkness, or "constant-value," horizontal slices (fig. 31 and color chart 3).
3. In terms of constant-intensity vertical cylindrical slices (and also for the enclosing cylinder which is not a slice), presented as if separated at yellow and spread flat (fig. 32 and color chart 4).

Second-Order Variations

The Pope color solid is a superb first-order statement of the basic nature of color appearance variability and color relations. It can facilitate general com-.

prehension, and serve as a mental construct for the convenience of artists, designers, architects, art critics, art historians, and others who use color or color concepts in their work.

To users of color it can be very helpful to have a simple and orderly conceptual framework within which color variables may be considered and dealt with free from the confusion of second-order or lesser variations. Artists and designers working with color need some easily remembered system of classification that can serve as a general guide when thinking about color. As Pope stressed, the creative user of color necessarily deals with approximations—and, as a practical matter, it is impossible even for color scientists to produce perfect color samples in terms of pigment materials.[4]

In order to present first-order trends with maximum clarity for the convenience of artists and designers, Pope stated that in a sense he had deliberately

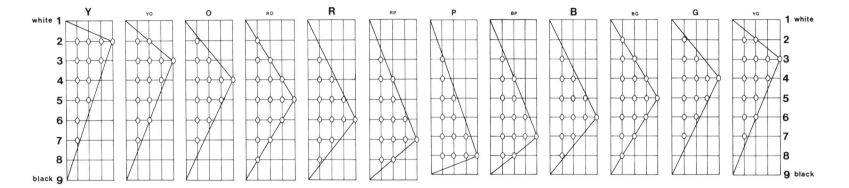

Figure 30
The 166 chromatic sampling points for
the Pope color solid as they appear on
the 12 constant-hue slices.

made his color solid inaccurate, just as the pitch of keyboard instruments (through the use of the well-tempered scale) is deliberately made inaccurate for the convenience of musicians.[5] By analogy the Pope color solid may be thought of as employing well-tempered scales. However, Pope's use of relative rather than absolute intensity should be viewed not as a form of tempering, but rather as a built-in feature of merit in its own right.*

Pope's emphasis on first-order trends was in no way the result of necessarily fuzzy thinking back in the days before adequate color measuring instruments had been developed. It has long been usual practice among scientists and others when describing phenomena of any kind to start by stressing the nature of dominant variability, and only thereafter proceeding to the consideration of second-order or lesser variables. Most

scientific "laws" are first-order statements of behavior.*

Two simple examples illustrate the concept of a first-order statement, and thus help to place the Pope color solid in proper perspective. The earth's ever-changing magnetic field can best be presented by first relating it to the earth's geographic axis, and only then going on to a consideration of its second-order changes over time, relative to that axis. To indicate the location of the Gulf Stream, its unchanging dominant or first-order trend will first be presented, after which the constantly changing and infinitely variable second-order departures therefrom can more effectively be dealt with—as exceptions to the general trend.

The problem with color is similar. It is only against a background of relative regularity that the nature of color irregularity can best be comprehended. The

*See this Supplement, pp. 118-120.

*See note 15 of "Introduction to Color."

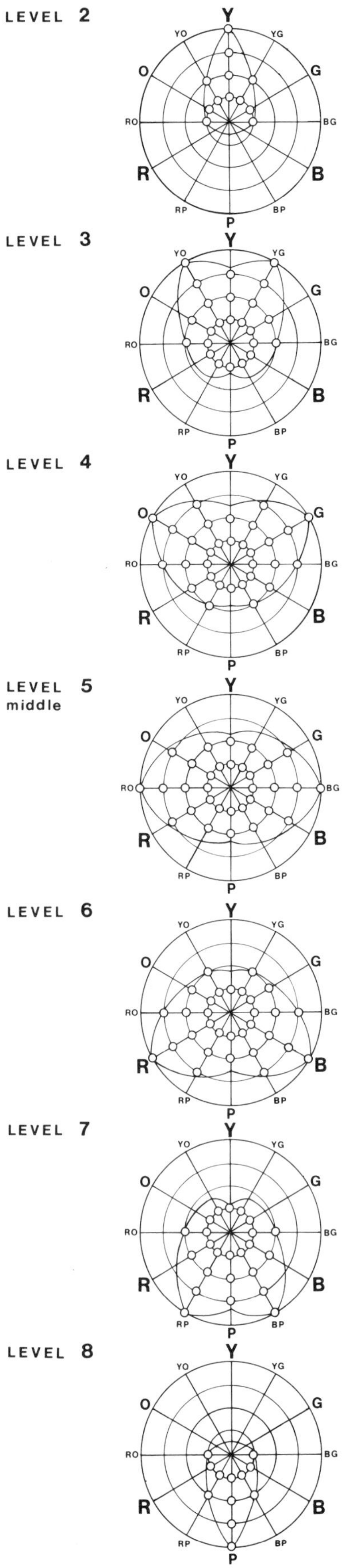

LEVEL **2**

LEVEL **3**

LEVEL **4**

LEVEL **5**
middle

LEVEL **6**

LEVEL **7**

LEVEL **8**

Figure 31
The 166 chromatic sampling points for the Pope color solid as they appear on the 7 constant-darkness or ("constant-value") slices.

basic variability of color, in spite of great variety in individual pigments or other colorants, tends to be remarkably regular and orderly in its nature. Thus the first-order color solid, as a statement of that variability, can be regular in form. The second-order trends of color must, however, also be dealt with and understood—and to that end let us now give them our consideration. In doing so it will be most convenient to concentrate particularly upon second-order trends relative to the constant-hue slices of the Pope color solid. If these are understood, the corresponding effects upon the constant-darkness and constant-intensity slices should be reasonably apparent.

As indicated earlier, the triangular shape of the constant-hue slices through the Pope color solid is meant to represent *approximately* the range of possibilities in terms of darkness (or "value") and intensity, when considered in relation to one another. When the actual facts for any hue (as measured in terms of samples) are charted against the assumed scales, the resulting shape of the constant-hue slice may at times depart significantly from that of a precise triangle. However, the outline of each constant-hue slice will always be at least roughly triangular in form.

There will generally be a sharply defined apex at the top (the white end of the neutral axis) and another at the bottom (the black end of the neutral axis). The third apex (representing high or 100% intensity) *may* be more or less rounded. The side of the triangle representing neutral will always be precisely straight and vertical, but each of the two remaining or oblique sides *may* curve significantly outward or inward.

For each hue the location of high or 100% intensity *may* at times depart significantly from the darkness level assumed by Pope.

The general trend of increasing darkness from yellows to purples (around either side of the Pope color circle) will always exist as a dominant first-order feature of color variability. In this connection, as stated by Pope, two second-order trends are particularly likely to be encountered: (1) purple of 100% intensity may fall somewhat higher than assumed, that is at a level less dark; (2) green of 100% intensity may fall substantially lower than assumed, that is, at a level more dark. These second-order deviations, though not necessarily present, may be likened to those of the magnetic North Pole or the Gulf Stream. They are usual and significant departures from the general or first-order trend. Once known, they are easy to remember and hard to forget. In figure 33 the V-shaped line shows the nature of the first-order trend in darkness, relative to hue, as presented in the Pope solid. The gray tone shows the area within which second-order deviations are most likely to occur.[6]

When plotting data measured from colored samples, still other departures from a strict triangular form may be encountered, such as possible reversal in the overall trend of an oblique side or minor irregularities in its shape. Such aberrations, however, are not likely to exist in actual color space—but only when attempting to measure and display color variability. They are usually the result of what is sometimes referred to as "noise"—due to imperfections in the preparation of the particular samples be-

Figure 32
The 166 chromatic sampling points for the Pope color solid as they appear on the high-intensity line and on the 3 constant-intensity slices—separated at Y and spread flat.

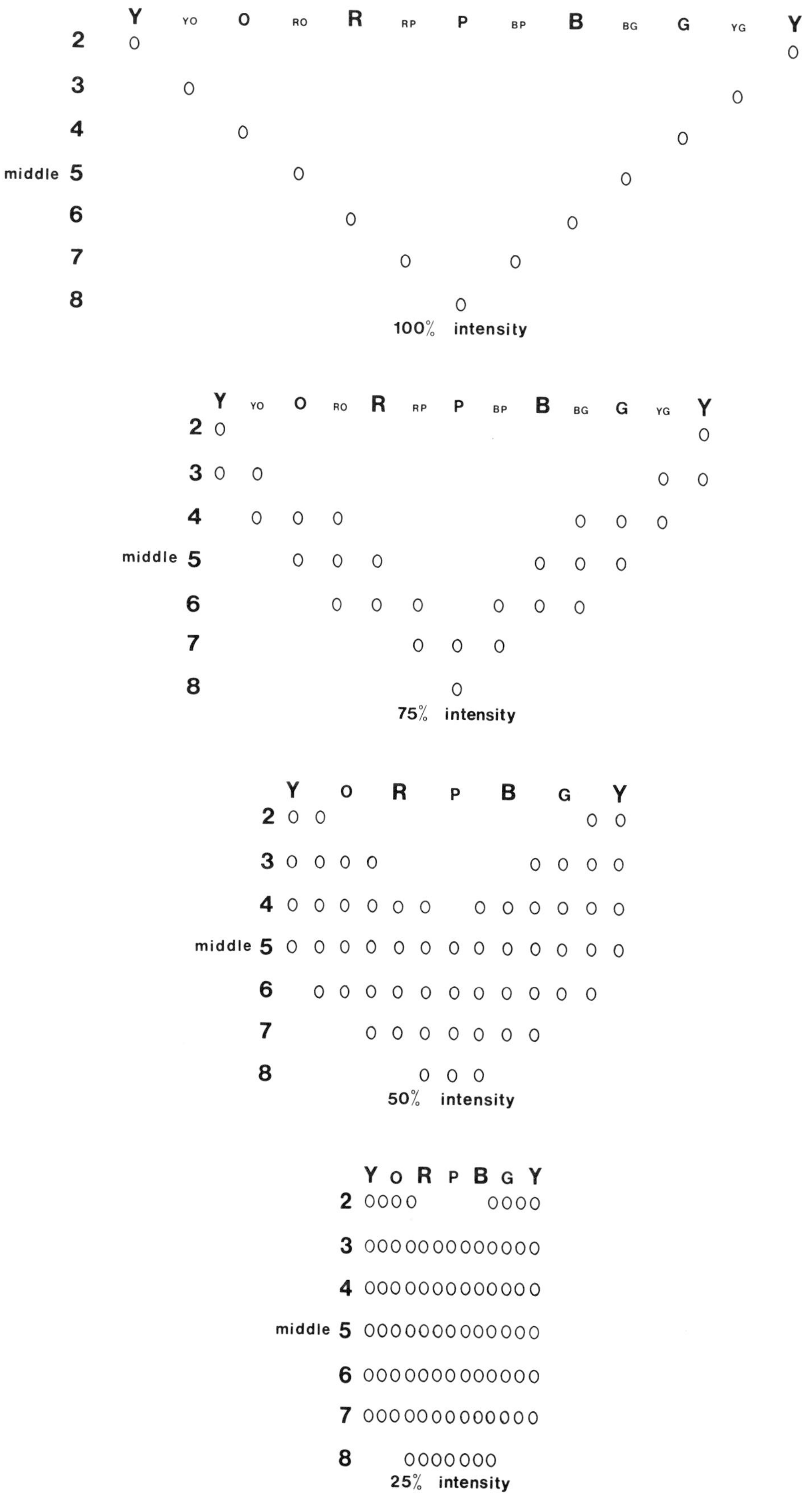

100% intensity

	Y	YO	O	RO	R	RP	P	BP	B	BG	G	YG	Y
2	O												O
3		O										O	
4			O								O		
middle 5				O						O			
6					O				O				
7						O		O					
8							O						

100% intensity

75% intensity

	Y	YO	O	RO	R	RP	P	BP	B	BG	G	YG	Y
2	O												O
3	O	O									G	O	
4		O	O	O					O	O	O		
middle 5			O	O	O			O	O	O			
6				O	O	O		O	O	O			
7						O	O	O					
8							O						

75% intensity

50% intensity

	Y		O		R		P		B		G		Y
2	O	O									O	O	
3	O	O	O	O					O	O	O	O	
4	O	O	O	O	O	O		O	O	O	O	O	O
middle 5	O	O	O	O	O	O	O	O	O	O	O	O	O
6		O	O	O	O	O	O	O	O	O	O	O	
7			O	O	O	O	O	O	O				
8				O	O	O							

50% intensity

25% intensity

Y o R p B g Y

2	O O O O						O O O O					
3	O O O O O O O O O O O O O O												
4	O O O O O O O O O O O O O O												
middle 5	O O O O O O O O O O O O O O												
6	O O O O O O O O O O O O O O												
7	O O O O O O O O O O O O O O												
8	O O O O O O O												

25% intensity

ing measured, inaccuracies in the overall measurement process, or inadequacies in the conversion procedure when going from instrument scales (which will typically be in the C.I.E. system) to the subjective scales of psychological color space. The last of these differences is likely to be especially serious.[7]

It would be helpful to be able to indicate with greater accuracy the probable nature and extent of the departure from first-order trends likely to result from second-order aberrations. It would be difficult, however, to make more precise (but still generally valid) statements than those made above and illustrated in figure 33, since the controlling facts will vary not only with the particular colorants used but also with the precise nature of the scales used in their analysis.* It *is* possible to show the facts for any particular set of colorants or color reproduction process in terms of any particular scales considered appropriate —but an attempt to do so here would be beyond the scope of this publication.

The important point is that while first-order trends can by definition be thought of as constant, second-order *color* trends cannot be so considered.

Features of the Pope Color Solid in Comparison with the Munsell System

Judged in terms of its objectives in relation to art, the Pope color solid possesses a number of features of particular merit. These can be conveniently highlighted through a comparison with the features of the widely used Munsell system of color notation.

*See this Supplement, pp. 115-120.

1. DARKNESS. For the light and dark extremes of neutral, the Pope system uses normally encountered white and black, in contrast to the theoretical but unachievable perfect white and black assumed in the Munsell system. In terms of Munsell goals the latter is preferable, but less satisfactory for the artist and designer—for whom the concept of theoretically perfect white or black has no reality.

In the Pope system there are eight steps in the darkness (or "value") scale, in contrast to the ten steps of the Munsell system. While the number of steps is not important in itself, by the use of eight steps Pope is able to demonstrate that very significant feature of color interrelationship: the first-order progression of increasing darkness for the seven high intensity hues from yellow to purple inclusive when going around either side of the color circle. In the Munsell system this relationship between hue and darkness is not featured and is only incidentally and crudely apparent. No high intensity surface is represented, and the highest intensity sampling points used provide no more than a rough clue as to its form. (Compare figs. 40 and 41 with figs. 2 and 35.)

2. HUE. The Pope solid is based on the traditional, easily grasped, and widely familiar 12-hue color circle—in terms of red, yellow, and blue as visual primaries. (See color chart 1.) This is in contrast to the 10-hue color circle of Munsell, which is based on the five colors of red, yellow, green, blue, and purple. In consequence, the Munsell hue circuit employs the somewhat

110

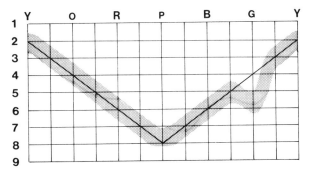

Figure 33
The high-intensity line of the Pope color solid. The shaded area shows where second-order deviations are most likely to occur.

awkward term of "yellow-red" to designate orange, and entirely omits verbal reference to red-orange and yellow-orange, which are referred to only as 10R and 10YR.

In the Munsell color circle only half as much space is allocated to hues between red and yellow as to those between yellow and blue, or blue and red. Yet the red-to-yellow (inclusive) portion of the hue circuit is of especially great visual and psychological significance to man. More than 40% of all chromatic color designations known to the English language relate to this portion.[8] In contrast, the traditional color circle, used by Pope, allocates the same amount of space to hues between red and yellow as to those between yellow and blue, or blue and red. As a helpful consequence of this procedure, purple (the darkest of the six basic hues) is directly opposite yellow (the lightest).[9]

The distinction between warm and cool hues is a useful one for reference purposes, but opinions tend to differ as to just where the breaks between the two should occur. In the Pope system the breaks are made at yellow and purple. Munsell, however, makes the breaks at green and red-purple (see the second chapter of Munsell's *A Color Notation*). Thus, he considers yellow-green to be warm and purple to be cool. If red is to be thought of as "hot" and blue as "cold" (the usual concept), it seems preferable to break at the halfway points between those two hues, as is done in the Pope system.

In both systems opposite hues on the color circle are only approximately complementary, but those of the Munsell system are better in this respect. (For the establishment of complementaries in the usual scientific sense the C.I.E. system is used.)

3. INTENSITY. The Pope system employs the more usual concept of relative intensity, rather than that of "chroma" used in the Munsell system. Intensity in the Munsell system is determined by the number of visually distinguishable steps that can be established between any given chromatic sample and a neutral of the same darkness. In terms of Munsell goals, "chroma" is an extremely useful unit of measurement since it is capable of being applied *independently* to any color sample. Artists and designers, however, are seldom concerned with color in any absolute sense, and have little reason to think in terms of visually distinguishable steps. For their purposes the concept of relative intensity is likely to be far more significant and more useful.

The Pope color solid, as befits a first-order statement, is smooth, regular, symmetrical, and unchanging in its exterior form. It is far more easily represented and remembered than the Munsell solid, which is irregular and variable in its exterior form.

The Pope solid stresses for the benefit of the artist, designer, and critic, the important relationship that exists between hue and characteristic hue darkness to be found at high intensity. The exterior form of the Munsell solid is indeterminate. It does not represent any meaningful concept—merely the highest chroma ratings that happen to be achievable at standard Munsell sampling points by Munsell standard chips available at any particular time—or by other specific colorants. In contrast, the form of the Pope solid is determined by the concept of high intensity, rather than by the maximum intensity achievable with particular colorants.

Based on presumed subjective constancy, the Pope solid is thus of fixed form, regardless of the particular colorants used, and regardless of the assumptions made as to what should constitute high intensity.

For users and viewers of colors in combination, as has been stressed repeatedly, color is fundamentally relative in nature; that is, color as seen in real life or in art is context-dependent. Until relatively recently, however, color scientists have tended to concentrate more upon colors seen one at a time against a neutral background.

The concept of the relative nature of color is basic to the Pope system: In the use of the 12-hue circuit relative to the three chosen primaries of red, yellow, and blue; in the use of relative rather than absolute white and black as the extremes of neutral; in the use of relative intensity; and finally, in the stress placed upon the first-order progression of increasing darkness around each side of the color circle in going from yellow to purple.

As among all color solids, the differences between Munsell and Pope may be accounted for primarily by the differences in the objectives of their designers. Neither Pope nor Munsell can be thought of as better than the other. Munsell sought to create a system for scoring the psychological variables of color, capable of indefinite expansion as more intense colorants (achieved by new dyes, fluorescence, or other means) might become available, and suitable for sampling color space at psychologically meaningful standardized locations. In terms of those very useful objectives, the Pope solid would be useless.

Pope had no interest in scoring color except broadly and in relative terms. He had no interest in standardization as such, and no need for an expandable color space. He sought to create a mental construct for the benefit of the artist, designer, and art critic. In a letter (April 24, 1973), Pope stated that his color solid was "designed to clarify thinking about color and color relations." He added, "It is the thinking that I would like emphasized." Of course, he had artists, designers, and art critics in mind, not color scientists, in regard to whom he felt unqualified to speak; and he was thinking in terms of surface color, produced by the traditional means he knew so well.[10]

Transforming and Scaling the Color Solid

Howard T. Fisher

THE SIMULTANEOUS DISPLAY OF
COLOR VARIABLES

By means of a simple geometric transformation, far more elementary than any used in map projections for displaying the surface of the earth, the three basic color variables—darkness (or "value"), hue, and intensity—can be simultaneously displayed, free of the visual confusions inherent to a cylindrical presentation on paper.

This result can be simply achieved by slitting vertically the surface of the enclosing cylinder at some convenient point (preferably at yellow), spreading it out flat, and then portraying upon it (by any suitable symbolism) the third variable of intensity. When the cylinder is thus flattened, the first two of the three color variables may be fully displayed at right angles to one another and without foreshortening. Changes in hue are represented horizontally and changes in darkness vertically, with white all across the top and black all across the bottom. These two color "dimensions" then correspond respectively with West to East and North to South in a Mercator map projection. The third variable of intensity, corresponding to "relief" or elevation on a typical map, can then be superimposed upon this base.

This type of solution was used in figure 22, which showed intensity on the surface of the Pope solid, the third variable being represented by numbers in circles. It could be represented graphically, however—with one possible solution assuming that the circles represented the tops of rods, which could then be drawn obliquely, with their height varied in proportion to the quantities to be represented. To minimize conflict among the rods, however, they might better be made of relatively small diameter, as shown in figure 34.

Since a continuous surface is being portrayed, a better solution would use a continuous type of symbolism, as for this same example in the oblique view of figure 2. As an alternative, a contoured representation of this might be used as shown in figure 35.[1]

As an alternative to such representations on paper, a three-dimensional model of rectangular shape could be used, in which case the enclosing cylindrical shape could be transformed, as in figure 36. The cylinder is first slit vertically at yellow and then progressively opened out, the neutral center being stretched in width to conform to the width of the cylinder's vertical surface. When the color solid is thus transformed, the slices for constant-hue, constant-darkness, and constant-intensity (shown earlier as figures 25, 26, and 27) now appear as shown in figures 37, 38, and 39.

Since the high relative intensity surface of the Pope color solid is smooth and regular, the transformations of that surface appear equally smooth and regular. In contrast, the corresponding absolute intensity (or "chroma") surface of the Munsell color solid is irregular in form. If displayed according to Munsell concepts in an oblique view or by contouring—in a manner corresponding to figures 2 and 35—it would appear as shown in figures 40 and 41.

In making such geometric transformations of "color space" we may use whatever scales appear most suitable. For the displays of Pope color space, the

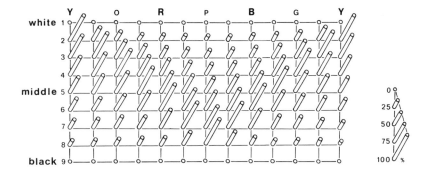

Figure 34
Standard sampling locations on the outer surface of the Pope color solid, separated at Y and flattened. Heights of rods indicate relative intensity, the highest rods representing 100%.

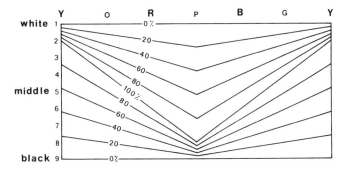

Figure 35
The continuous outer surface of the Pope color solid, separated at Y and flattened. Contour lines indicate the magnitude of relative intensity.

scales discussed on the next page were used. For those of Munsell color space, the standard scales of the Munsell system were used.[2] The major differences in the Munsell surface as compared with the Pope surface result from the fact that absolute intensity is being represented by the Munsell surface. The minor irregularities result from the data being at standard sampling locations.

If, instead of displaying a continuous phenomenon as in the illustrative examples just considered, we wish to portray facts about a limited number of specific colors, we might employ discrete symbols to represent the magnitudes of the intensities. By way of illustration let us consider the Guston painting, *Summer, 1954* (no. 1). To analyze the color Carpenter selected thirteen specific and relatively small sampling locations which he felt to be particularly significant. When scored according to our assumed scales for the Pope system, the colors at those locations might then be graphically communicated as shown in figure 42.[3]

In the two parts to figure 42, as in the previous color space transformations, the hue and darkness of each color is represented by the location of the symbols. Intensity is then represented by the size of the symbols—that is, the areas of the circles or the heights of the rods.[4] As may be seen from the symbolism, two of the thirteen sampling locations share the same hue and darkness—although different in intensity.

It would appear probable, however, that color schemes in art may only seldom be appropriately represented thus by colors narrowly defined, and as found at a limited number of sampling locations. Hence more generalized symbol-

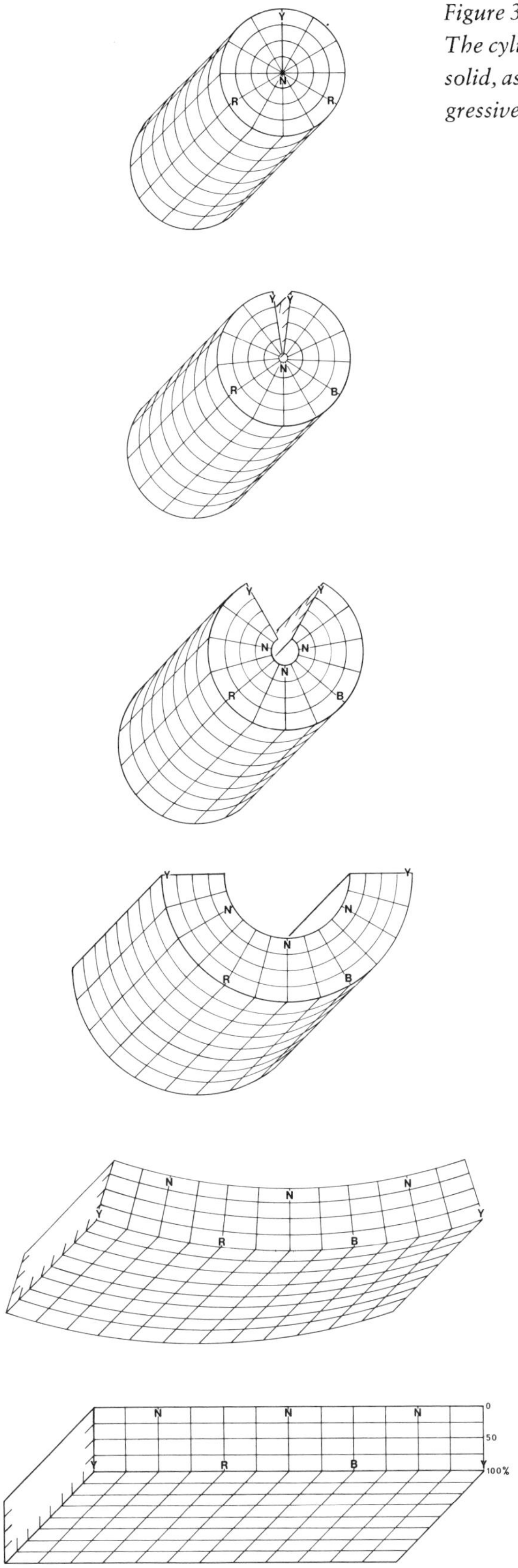

Figure 36
The cylinder enclosing the Pope color solid, as if cut at yellow and then progressively stretched out straight.

ism will usually prove more appropriate than symbolism of this discrete type. Figure 43 illustrates the use of such symbolism—of a contour type achieved by interpolation. Directly corresponding symbolism but of an oblique-view type was shown in figure 1. This type of display permits showing only the maximum intensity for each hue and darkness combination.

While such more generalized "color scores" can be drawn by hand rather laboriously, the computer is capable of producing them both rapidly and cheaply and with consistent accuracy. Figures 1, 3, 4, and 40 were all so produced.[5] In each case the display is presented in isometric projection as if viewed from the lower left looking in at an angle of 45°. However, they might have been presented in true perspective, or from any other direction and angle.

The major advantage of this type of three-variable color score, as compared to the normal cylindrical display, is that it shows with great clarity simultaneous relationships in terms of all three basic color qualities. Two-dimensional slices through the color solid can show only two qualities at most.[6]

The major disadvantage of this type of display as compared to the normal cylindrical method is that distance in the display may be less representative of visual distance. For example, red and blue of low intensity and middle darkness would appear far apart in the display, while in reality and within the Pope solid they would be rather close together in appearance (fig. 44). Two-dimensional representations, however, may present similar problems. For example, a horizontal two-dimensional display in terms

of hue and intensity would show a very light yellow-orange and a very dark red-orange as rather close together, when in reality and within the Pope solid they would be far apart in appearance (fig. 45). For these colors a vertical two-dimensional display in terms of darkness and intensity (as in figs. 7 and 10) would show no distinction in terms of hue. In contrast, a three-variable color score would reveal the true situation with considerable accuracy.[7]

SCALES

In order to be able to make meaningful comparisons among alternative color schemes used in works of art it is, of course, necessary to employ the same scales in each case. The following discussion considers problems involved in establishing such scales, and describes the particular scales used in the preparation of the various figures that have been provided (other than for Munsell color space, illustrated and explained in the previous section).

In the case of two-dimensional diagrams for other than the paintings of Guston, Turner, and Homer, the evaluations were made by Carpenter without specific reference to color samples.

The Darkness Scale

Pope proposed the use of a darkness (or "value") scale in terms of neutral, divided into eight visually equal steps between white and black. He did not specify the nature of the background to be assumed, what white or black to use as the end points of the gray scale, or what size of samples and what spacing to employ.

115

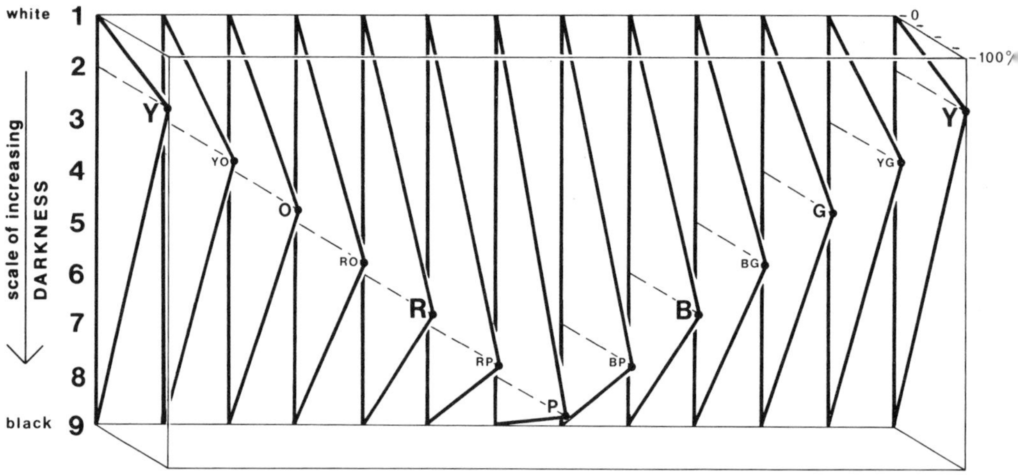

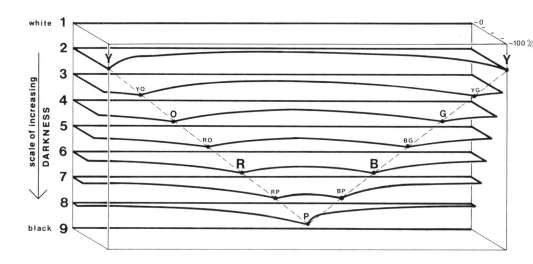

Figure 37
The 12 constant-hue slices through the transformed Pope color solid.

Figure 38
The 7 constant-darkness (or "constant-value") slices through the transformed Pope color solid. High intensity is shown by the dashed line.

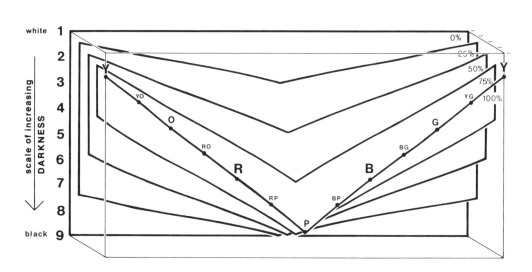

Figure 39
The 3 constant-intensity slices through the transformed Pope color solid (plus the neutral "base" of 0% and the high-intensity line of 100%).

From charts that he and some of his students made (in the possession of the Fogg Art Museum) and from the color charts that appeared in later books, it is reasonably clear what he had in mind, but how the results were related in any valid sense to the "complex fields" of art is not clear.

The influence of the above-mentioned variables, and also of the nature and brightness of the viewing light, were far less well understood in the period of Pope's most creative work. He fully appreciated their importance, but in regard to his darkness scale he would be likely to say, "What difference does it make, since color appearance is all of a relative nature?"

Unfortunately—in this instance at least—it does make a difference, since the relationships which Ross and Pope established between darkness and the characteristic high intensity of hues have far greater validity with some darkness scales than others. Also, if we are to analyze works of art according to Pope concepts, and be able to compare one with another, it is essential to use a single darkness scale, even if no one scale performs equally well under all circumstances. Our problem is thus to choose that one darkness scale that will best serve the purposes of the Pope color solid.

With the present state of knowledge we might do worse than to adopt today's most widely employed darkness scale, used with the Munsell system and developed with the aid of the National Bureau of Standards. Widely accepted today, it possesses an especially significant virtue for our purposes: the Ross-Pope concept of the hue-darkness relationship (one of the more useful features of the Pope color solid) proves to be most valid when such a darkness scale is employed.

Perhaps unfortunately, modern research suggests that this scale, if judged in terms of the goal of visually equal spacing, is most suitable when the background is very dark. Nonetheless, at least until such time as more research can be devoted to the problems of darkness scales in terms of complex fields, it would appear to provide our best solution. This is especially the case since visually equal spacing is not a primary goal and is not achievable in any case under varying conditions or for the color solid as a whole.

Aided by consultation with the Rochester Institute of Technology's Graphic Arts Research Center, we have also assumed that relative white and black in the Pope solid may be reasonably represented by Munsell "values" 9.25/ and 2/ respectively (corresponding to "Y" values of 84.20% and 3.13% in terms of the C.I.E. system.)[8]

The Hue Scale

The Pope color solid is based on the use of twelve hues, derived by successive subdivision between red, yellow, and blue—the three traditional visual primaries. When diagrammed, these are spaced in a circle at equal intervals (like the hour positions on the face of a clock).

In naming the hues, Pope used the word *violet* rather than the word *purple.* Violet is present in the visible spectrum, while purple is not, and violet is also more toward blue than the color Pope intended. Hence we have adopted the term *purple,* used also by Munsell and others, as more appropriate.

Figure 40
The outer surface of the Munsell color solid, separated at Munsell red-purple and stretched out straight. Munsell hue runs horizontally, Munsell "value" runs vertically, and Munsell "chroma" runs obliquely (as "relief" or "elevation").

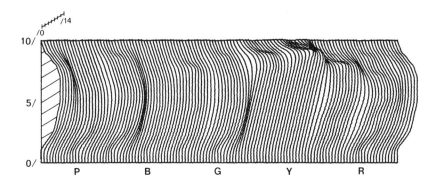

Figure 41
The outer surface of the Munsell color solid, separated at Munsell red-purple and stretched out straight. Munsell hue runs horizontally, Munsell "value" runs vertically, and Munsell "chroma" is shown by the use of contouring.

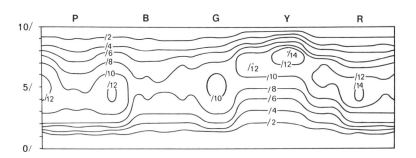

Given these assumptions, it is still necessary to decide exactly what hues best represent the names we use. Fortunately, some years ago at the suggestion of the Inter-Society Color Council, an extensive study of this problem was undertaken by the National Bureau of Standards. Its results have been used in preparing the color scores shown in figures 1, 3, and 4.[9]

The hues of the Pope system thus established are in part substantially different from those assumed for the Munsell system. This is especially true in the case of blue, which in the Munsell system is far more greenish. Munsell yellow is also rather greenish (especially darker yellow). As defined in Munsell notation, the ISCC-NBS hues employed for the Pope solid are as follows: Y (4Y), YO (9YR), O (4.5YR), RO (9.5R), R (4.5R), RP (3RP), P (6P), BP (9PB), B (3PB), BG (10BG), G (6G), YG (5GY).

The Intensity Scale
The Pope color solid uses the concept of relative intensity. As mentioned earlier, people tend to associate the concept of hue and the basic names of hues (yellow, orange, red, purple, blue, and green) with the highest intensity commonly encountered with each such hue, and to judge lesser intensities for the same hue in relation to it.

When judged in terms of common experience, hues of high intensity thus appear to possess a certain consistency—a certain sense of shared identity and belonging together. This is not the case, at least to anything like the same extent, among hues of uniform "chroma" in the Munsell system. The validity of this statement can easily be demonstrated by procuring and comparing two sets of Munsell chips: One, a set of uniform relative intensity (5Y 8.5/14, 5YR 7/14, 5R 5/14, 5P 3/10, 5B 5/8, 5G

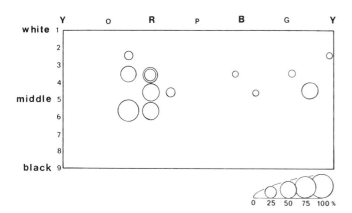

Figure 42
The color scheme of the Guston painting represented by discrete symbols, based on colors at 13 selected locations. Hue and darkness are shown by symbol position, and intensity by the overall areas of the circles or the heights of the rods.

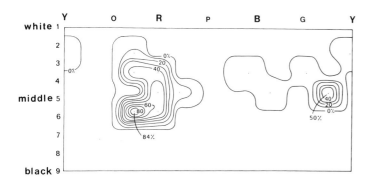

Figure 43
The color scheme of the Guston painting represented in a generalized manner by the use of contouring (based on colors at selected locations, shown by dots).

6/10), and the other set of uniform "chroma" intensity (5Y 8.5/8, 5YR 7/8, 5R 5/8, 5P 3/8, 5B 5/8, 5G 6/8). The former will appear to most people to possess an internal consistency or unity far more basic and obvious in terms of common visual experience than the latter. Only persons trained in the use of "chroma" as a rating scale would be likely, for example, to be undisturbed by the difference to be found in the second set between the high relative intensity of the green and blue samples and the low relative intensity of the orange and red samples. To most persons, apparently, the latter tend to appear almost "dirty" in marked contrast to the "clean" effect of the former.

For the purpose of illustrating the color circle, it would appear that the concept of relative intensity has been traditionally and generally employed. That is, hues of characteristic high inten-

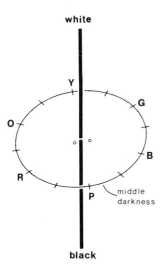

Figure 44
Diagram showing the positions within
the Pope solid of red and blue of low
intensity and middle darkness.

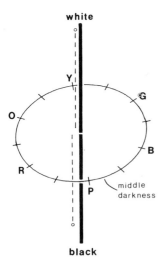

Figure 45
Diagram showing the positions within
the Pope solid of light yellow-orange
and dark red-orange. The dashed lines
running to middle darkness serve to
establish hue and intensity.

sity have been used insofar as possible and all have been placed at a uniform distance from the center of the color circle (as in color chart 1). In contrast, the concept of "chroma"—Munsell's special solution to meet his particular needs—seems to have been used in no other system.

When the concept of relative intensity is used, the scale for each hue is based upon high intensity for that hue, which in each case is set equal to 100%. All samples of less than high intensity for the same hue are then established in relation to that. By painstaking research this could be done by direct visual means, but since absolute intensity scores in terms of Munsell "chroma" are at this time generally available (or readily determinable), matters can be greatly facilitated by their use. Unfortunately, however, no research seems ever to have been undertaken to establish the most suitable ratings to represent the various high intensities.[10]

We would like to know the typical "chroma" ratings of the colors people have in their minds when, in the normal course of events, they might visualize surface colors of high intensity. Since that might be difficult to determine, the logic of the situation would appear to call for knowledge of the most intense surface colors which people in the normal course of their lives are likely to encounter. It is in relation to these that less intense examples of the same hues are presumably judged.

For this purpose it might appear appropriate to use the highest intensities available among the glossy color chips of the Munsell system. Unfortunately, however, for some hues these fall short

of surface color intensities widely encountered in ordinary experience. For example, the intensities to be found in colored illustrations printed by the 4-color lithographic process are, for a number of hues, considerably more intense than those to be found in the Munsell collection—though for some other hues they are substantially less intense.

To serve present needs, and until more revealing research can be carried out (including study of the possible influence of variable darkness), we have assumed as the basis for our computations the highest "chroma" ratings to be found in the combined Munsell and four-color gamuts.[11]

As a partial check on the logic of this approach we have investigated the highest absolute intensities to be found among the samples available for the ISCC-NBS system (issued by the National Bureau of Standards) and for the Ostwald system (as presented in the *Color Harmony Manual*). Only the red chip for the ISCC-NBS system and the blue-purple chip for the Ostwald system were more than slightly higher in intensity, but even in those cases the difference was still rather small (about 9% and 15% higher respectively). All other samples were either almost identical or less intense. Overall, the Ostwald chips tended to be much less intense than with the combined Munsell and four-color gamut.[12]

Notes

Bibliographies

Index

Notes

AN INTRODUCTION TO COLOR

1. Color can result from flicker alone, although color so caused is seen so rarely that few people are aware of the possibility. For example, when certain black and white patterns are rotated on a turntable and viewed in ordinary daylight, sensations of color will result. Such color sensations are identical to those caused by variations in wavelength, and are equally real or true colors. See Leon Festinger, Mark R. Allyn, and Charles W. White, "The Perception of Color with Achromatic Stimulation," *Vision Research,* 11 (1971), 591-612; and Josef Cohen and Donald A. Gordon, "The Prevost-Fechner-Benham Subjective Colors," *Psychological Bulletin,* 46 (March 1949), 97-136.

2. So-called color-blind persons usually experience sensations of color, but in a way that is substantially different from the sensations felt by persons with vision lying within the normal range. About 8.5% of males but less than about 0.5% of females are partially color-blind. Only a very small percentage of persons are totally blind to color, in the sense of perceiving the world monochromatically.

3. Obviously, this is a situation that would be difficult if not impossible to produce with perfection even under laboratory conditions. It would also be necessary to imagine that the eye and brain operating under such circumstances would do so in such a way as to yield an absolutely uniform impression of color over the entire field of vision, as only thus would we receive the sensation of *one* color.

4. When the light entering the eye is composed of certain very particular combinations of wavelengths, available in certain very particular combinations of strength, the resulting color will be achromatic. Two wavelengths only are sufficient to produce this result, if they are what is known as complementary in terms of the C.I.E. system used by color scientists (described briefly in note 16). Any number of wavelengths may, however, be involved.

5. A few materials, such as polished metals or substances of regular crystalline form, have the power of selectively reflecting wavelengths of light from their exposed outer surfaces only. The word *surface* in this discussion is meant to convey a somewhat less narrow meaning.

6. Light is a form of energy. When it is absorbed by a material the energy is converted into heat, and the temperature of the material is increased. For example, when sunlight falls upon a dull black surface almost all the light is absorbed, with a resulting noticeable increase in temperature.

   Mention should be made of the phenomenon of fluorescence, which results when light of a certain wavelength is converted by a surface to light of a longer wavelength. The original light is usually in the invisible ultraviolet range, with the light emitted in the visible range. Fluorescent pigments or inks make possible colors of greater than usual intensity, and it is for this reason that they are frequently employed for high visibility garments or for advertising signs. In recent years such pigments have occasionally been used in art, but the problems are of such a special nature that they will not be considered here.

7. We will also assume that the eye has had sufficient time to become adapted to the level of brightness provided by the viewing light, and to the background or conditions surrounding the object being observed.

   In analyzing the colors of translucent art objects in contrast to opaque objects such as paintings, one special problem is likely to arise. With translucent objects (stained glass, for example), levels of hue intensity may be encountered that are far greater than any experienced with surface color. This is, of course, particularly likely to be the case if the far side of the object is exposed to direct sunlight. In terms of the concept of relative intensity, shortly to be considered, it would for such works of art be necessary to relate to a "high intensity" appropriate to transmitted light. In other words, when looking at a stained glass window one would need to judge intensity in relation to the maximum intensity normally encountered with transmitted light rather than in relation to the maximum intensity normally encountered with reflected light from surfaces.

8. Dispersal is also the source of colors produced by such things as oil slicks and the grooves of long-playing phonograph records.

9. For corresponding reasons the term *darkness* is frequently employed in the graphic arts field—as, for example, by the color scientists of the Rochester Institute of Technology's Graphic Arts Research Center.

10. Concepts vary widely as to what hues should be considered primary. While not important for our purposes in relation to art, a few observations may be of interest. Red, yellow, and blue have probably been most generally accepted as primary, perhaps because the usual pigments employed to produce those distinctive hues are capable of being mixed to produce all intermediate hues (even if of low intensity). Some students of color prefer red, yellow, and blue, *plus green*. In the system developed by A. H. Munsell (to be discussed) red, yellow, green, blue, and purple are the basic hues employed. In the additive process, red, green, and blue are the most useful primaries, and hence these are the colors used in television sets. With the 4-color printing process, yellow, magenta, and cyan are the most effective hues. In relation to the spectrum, students of physics are usually told of the seven hue designations employed by Newton: red, orange, yellow, green, blue, indigo, and violet. Newton included indigo because he was a mystic and wanted to make the number of hues equal to the "magic" number 7. He omitted purple (since it is not in the spectrum) but probably included violet as that hue which along with red defines the limits of visible color.

11. Just as North is usually placed at the top of maps, so in diagramming "color space" it is customary to place white at the top and black at the bottom. Hence, in arranging hues it would appear appropriate to place yellow nearest to white at the top.

12. Richard I. Land, research scientist at Harvard University, in commenting on this statement has written: "Color is the result of decoding a scene in context. It is an unstable perception, in that it is context dependent. A red surface looks white in a uniform red light. Color is weak at best in isolation and really *cannot* in any perceptual sense be defined that way. It must be in context—preferably a *rich real world*, not the impoverished psychophysical spot/surround situation used in much color research. All present theories of color vision depend on interaction in a real spatially defined system."

13. B. F. Skinner, *Beyond Freedom and Dignity* (New York: A. A. Knopf, 1971), p. 103. Red appears as an "after-image" when one has been looking intently at blue-green, its approximate complementary. For artichokes, see *Science,* December 1, 1972, p. 988.

14. For a discussion of color constancy (defined in a somewhat broader sense), and various theories regarding it, see Jacob Beck, *Surface Color Perception* (Ithaca, N.Y.: Cornell University Press, 1972).

15. The *International Dictionary of Physics and Electronics* (1961) defines first-order theory as "Any theory which involves only the most important terms . . . ." It then adds the statement that "Many physical theories are of first order."

The Pope color solid may be defined in mathematical terms as consisting of all points given by the parametric expression

$$P = \left(\frac{5}{2}\gamma\alpha, \ \theta, \ -\alpha\frac{6}{\pi}\,|\,\pi - \theta\,| \right) + \left\{ \begin{array}{c} (0, 0, 1 + 7\,\alpha) \\ (0, 0, 9 - \alpha) \end{array} \right\}$$

for $0 \leqslant \alpha \leqslant 1, 0 \leqslant \gamma < 1, 0 \leqslant \theta \leqslant 2\pi$

where P is any point within or on the surface of the solid, θ is the hue angle measured counterclockwise from yellow, and α and δ are independent parameters assuming all values from 0 to 1 inclusive. Setting $\delta = 1$ gives the surface of the solid, while $\delta < 1$ gives the interior of the solid. The high intensity curve corresponds to setting $\delta = 1$ and $\alpha = 1$. We are indebted to Dr. Arther S. Priver, applied mathematician and computer consultant, Wellesley Hills, Massachusetts, for this formulation.

16. A brief mention of the principal color order systems now in use may be of interest. The most widely known is the Munsell system of color notation. It has as its primary objectives the psychological scoring of color qualities and the offering of illustrative color swatches (usually referred to as "chips") at Munsell standard sampling locations. See the *Supplement*, pp. 110-112, for a discussion of the Munsell system as compared with the Pope system. See also figures 40 and 41 and the related discussion.

In Munsell notation, scores for darkness (called "value") are followed by a slash line (thus, 5/), while scores for absolute intensity (called "chroma") are preceded by a slash (thus, /10). When the two scores are written together, a single slash only is used (thus, 5/10, to indicate the combination of Munsell "value" 5 and "chroma" 10). Conversion between the Pope and Munsell systems can be easily achieved, given a decision as to the scaling to be employed for the Pope system. (See the *Supplement*, pp. 115-120.) For an introduction to the work of Munsell, beyond that to be given in this publication, see Albert H. Munsell, *A Grammar of Color . . .*, edited . . . by Faber Birren (New York: Van Nostrand Reinhold Company, 1969). Up-to-date information regarding the Munsell system and products illustrating it can be obtained from the Munsell Color Division, Kollmorgen Corporation, 2441 North Calvert Street, Baltimore, Maryland, 21218.

The Ostwald system, used less today than formerly, will be described briefly, below, in note 19.

The C.I.E. system (usually so identified, after its sponsor the *Commission Internationale de l'Eclairage* or International Commission on Illumination) exists primarily for the graphing of psychophysical data relative to color. The system and its rationale are too complex for explanation here, but a few key points should be mentioned. Its three basic dimensions carry the designations x, y, and Y. The first two determine location on a standard coordinate grid measured from the lower left, horizontally for x (designating red), and vertically for y (designating green). The variable of Y (designating lightness-darkness) is measured vertically from theoretically perfect black at the bottom to theoretically perfect white at the top. However, this parameter is usually noted numerically rather than represented graphically. Conversion between the C.I.E. and Munsell systems may be achieved by means of charts plus arithmetic interpolation. Computer programs also exist for the purpose, and information regarding them may be procured from Professor Fred W. Billmeyer, Jr., Color Measurement Laboratory Rensselaer Polytechnic Institute at Troy, New York. (A simplified graphic method for making such conversions has been developed by the writer and is currently in the process of refinement.)

The 3-color process (somewhat obsolete for printing but now being used for office machine copying) is easily represented in terms of ink mixtures by a color solid in the form of a cube balanced on one corner. Systematic mixtures of cyan and magenta appear on one of the three top surfaces, with yellow and cyan on another, and yellow and magenta on the third. Combinations of all three inks then occupy the remaining three surfaces and the interior.

The 4-color process (that most widely employed today in printing) cannot be shown in an orderly manner in terms of ink mixtures by a single color solid, since four independent dimensions are involved (for yellow, magenta, cyan, and black). In this connection Carl E. Foss recently developed a new concept, available as the Foss Color System from the Graphic Arts Technical Foundation in Pittsburgh (under license from the Munsell organization). In this system of color appearance the 4-color process is illustrated in a rational manner.

Various procedures involving the systematic mixture of a limited number of colorants (pigments or dyes) have been developed, most frequently in terms of proprietary paints. Pigment mixing, however, involves technical problems of great complexity, and the results achieved will depend heavily upon the chemical nature of the particular pigments used.

For further information on these color systems, and descriptions of others too numerous to consider here, see Dean B. Judd and Günter Wyszecki, *Color in Business, Science and Industry* (2d ed., 1963); and Günter Wyszecki, "Colorimetry," in Raymond A. Eynard, ed., *Color: Theory and Imaging Systems* (Washington, D.C.: Society of Photographic Scientists and Engineers, 1973), pp. 24-44.

17. This statement is based on conversations with Pope. Ross and Pope were colleagues, close neighbors, and friends over many years, and Pope repeatedly acknowledged his dependence on ideas developed by Ross. It was in this connection that he jokingly referred to objections Ross raised to the incorporation of his color scales and triangles into the Pope color solid.

Ross and Munsell (who was some five years younger) had known each other at least since 1892, when they went sketching together in Venice and talked over the possibility of a "systematic color scheme for painters." See Dorothy Nickerson, "History of the Munsell Color System and Its Scientific Application," *Journal of the Optical Society of America,* 30 (December 1940), 575-586. Yet according to Pope, Ross was unsympathetic to the idea of a color solid, a concept then being used by Munsell. He apparently felt that at best it was an unnecessary complication.

18. Pope was modest and even apologetic in appraising his color solid. In his description of it he referred repeatedly to its defects, inaccuracies, and limitations. This was consistent with his retiring temperament, but also may have resulted from his feeling somewhat on the defensive in view of the tremendous and well-earned success being achieved by Munsell's increasingly sophisticated and scientifically trained followers. The two systems, however, were designed to serve quite different objectives.

19. Ostwald's color solid achieved wide recognition, especially in Europe. It took the form of a regular double cone, with high intensity for each of its 24 hues at the apex of an equilateral triangle. As with those of Ross and Pope, it was based on relative intensity. The darkness scale of Ostwald's neutral axis was of logarithmic type appropriate to visual differences judged against a very dark background—somewhat similar to that of Munsell. Other than along its neutral axis, however, darkness as a basic color dimension was ignored. For more information see Wilhelm Ostwald, *The Color Primer . . . ,* edited . . . by Faber Birren (New York: Van Nostrand Reinhold Company, 1969); and the *Color Harmony Manual* (4th ed., 1958) issued by the Container Corporation of America, Chicago, Illinois; also the special symposium of papers on the Ostwald Color System in *Journal of the Optical Society of America,* 34 (July 1944).

20. If visually equal spacing within a color solid were possible, two advantages would result. First, the contrast or difference between any two or more colors would be known if the locations of those colors within the color solid were known. Second, if one were to

sample the color solid at uniformly spaced locations, one could be certain that for any given number of samples the most representative collection of samples would be achieved. For these reasons designers of color solids have long sought to achieve visually equal spacing.

To illustrate the problem, there is probably no one darkness scale (even for any given set of viewing conditions) that can be applied equally to all intensities of all hues. Nonetheless, even though perfection as to equal spacing is improbable, the quest for the nearest possible approach to perfection continues unabated. From the viewpoint of the artist, designer, and art critic, however, there is a fundamental dilemma: Any geometry that is sufficiently simple and orderly to serve as a mental construct for the purposes of thinking broadly about color will not have sampling points that are equally spaced in visual terms—while any geometry that achieves maximum uniformity in terms of visually equal spacing will not be sufficiently simple and orderly to serve as a mental construct. By way of example, for thinking purposes it is helpful or perhaps even essential to be able to visualize slices through the color solid which are of equal hue, equal darkness, or equal intensity. Such slices should preferably be planes, but must at least be geometrically comprehensible (such as the cylindrical slices used in the Pope and Munsell systems for constant intensity).

For the artist, designer, and art critic at least, the goal of ready comprehension in terms of basic visual qualities is a far more significant goal than that of equality in terms of visual spacing (for which the creative artist and designer really have little or no concern). A disordered three-dimensional color space in terms of hue, darkness, and intensity would be even worse than a disordered two-dimensional clock face with minutes and hours spaced unequally in geometric terms in pursuit of the goal of psychologically equal spacing—as perhaps with wider minutes during times for eating or loving and narrower minutes during times for sleeping.

Unfortunately, no publication has yet been issued on the status of the intensive search for visually equal spacing currently being made by the Colorimetry Committee of C.I.E. and also the Committee on Uniform Color Scales of the Optical Society of America.

21. Faber Birren, in *The Story of Color* (Westport, Conn.: Crimson Press, 1941), p. 256, illustrates and briefly describes a color solid which somewhat resembles that of Pope (to which he refers as being of "the same form"). Actually, the difference between the two would appear to be rather fundamental, since the Birren solid seems to have no consistent scale of intensity. For example, red-orange and green are placed the same distance from the neutral axis, which would be correct for relative intensity, though other colors, particularly yellow and violet, are placed far closer.

In speaking of color solids in general, Birren makes the following very revealing comment: "the attempt to organize the world of color in a systematic way is vital to progress. The purpose is to make order out of chaos and to assist *both science and art* in searching the medium more thoroughly, having at their command *a well charted map of exploration.*"

We believe the emphasis (which has been added) wisely stresses the fact that there can be varying goals, that the search for truth as to color space (being rooted in man's perceptions) is probably an endless task, and that well charted, even if less than perfect, "maps" are essential to progress.

COLOR IN ART

1. All remarks attributed to Pope come from the 1949 edition of *The Language of Drawing and Painting.*

2. Plates from Albers' book, *Interaction of Color* (New Haven: Yale University Press, 1963), demonstrate the relative nature of color experience, and how one must be ready to modify color judgment radically under differing conditions.

3. E. H. Gombrich, *Art and Illusion* (New York: Pantheon Books, 1956), p. 90.

4. Cennino Cennini, *Il Libro dell' Arte* (The Craftsman's Handbook), trans. by D. V. Thompson (New Haven: Yale University Press, 1933).

5. S. P. Cowardin has devised the simple descriptive forms "up-model," "down-model," and "hue shift." See his "Some Aspects of Color in Fifteenth-Century Florentine Painting," unpub. Ph.D. diss., Harvard University, 1963.

6. Letter from Pissarro to Durand-Ruel, in John Rewald, *The History of Impressionism* (New York: Museum of Modern Art, 1946), p. 383.

7. In a conversation with Cézanne recorded by Joachin Gasquet, in Bernard Dorival, *Cézanne,* trans. by H. H. A. Thackwaite (New York: Continental Book Center, 1948) p. 102.

THE FORM OF THE COLOR SOLID

1. For a technical discussion of the numerous and frequently conflicting terms used in color work, see Deane B. Judd and Günter Wyszecki, *Color in Business, Science, and Industry,* 2nd ed. (New York: John Wiley & Sons, 1963).

2. The scale concepts were presented in Ross's *Theory of Pure Design* (1907).

3. With a view to equalizing visual spacing within the color solid insofar as possible, Pope recommended making the width of the constant-hue triangles approximately two-and-one-half eighths (or 31.25%) of their height. When the enclosing cylinder of the Pope color solid is slit at Y and flattened out, this causes the horizontal length to be almost exactly twice the height. For graphic work by computer slightly different proportions may be used in order to fit computer spacing requirements.

    High intensities for the twelve hues are not necessarily all of the same intensity when judged in other scales. For example, 100% red-orange will normally be far more intense in "chroma" terms than 100% blue. With Munsell glossy chips, the maximum absolute intensity or "chroma" scores for those hues (as defined by Munsell) would be /16.5 and /10 respectively.

4. The difficulty is well illustrated by the continuing presence among Munsell chips of color samples that fail by a substantial margin to conform to their designations. In the 1970 listing of Munsell glossy chips there are 153 such samples.

5. *Webster's Third New International Dictionary* defines *temperament* as "the system or process of slightly modifying the musical intervals of the pure scale to produce a set of compromise tones consisting of twelve fixed tones to the octave and thus permit modulations without the use of an inconveniently large number of distinctions in pitch. . . ."

6. If constant-hue triangles pursuant to what are called the "MacAdam limits" are examined, it can be seen that high-intensity green falls at the lower limit of high-intensity blue-green (and also blue). The centers of gravity of the blue-green and green constant-hue triangles fall at almost identically the same darkness level (Munsell "values" 5.19/ and 5.22/ respectively). There would thus appear to be no inherent necessity for a reversal or dip at green. For the "MacAdam limits" see Dorothy Nickerson and Sidney M. Newhall, "A Psychological Color Solid," *Journal of the Optical Society of America,* 33 (1943), 419-422.

    When the high intensity for any hue falls at a darkness level other than that assumed (as mentioned above in the case of purple and green), the highest possible intensity at the assumed darkness level will necessarily be less high. This can prove doubly troublesome when attempting to illustrate first-order trends with actual chromatic samples, and there would appear to be no entirely satisfactory solution. The best solution, and the one used in preparing color charts 2, 3, and 4, is to treat the highest intensity at the darkness level assumed in the Pope color solid as if it were 100%.

7. In 1943 the Munsell color solid, developed over a period of many years and before modern color measuring devices had been invented, was given intensive scrutiny by the Optical Society of America acting through its Subcommittee on the Spacing of the Munsell Colors. As was to be expected, when instrument-derived scores for the Munsell chips were plotted according to the C.I.E. system, irregularities were found to exist. To correct these, smooth curves were developed and the samples rescored accordingly. The term "renotation" is used to refer to the new scores, still in use today. Unfortunately, however, those responsible for the replotting seem to have concentrated upon the behavior of the data horizontally in terms of the two-dimensional constant-darkness slices, with little or no regard to behavior in the third dimension. When the information is plotted vertically, in terms of constant-hue or constant-"chroma" slices, rather startling aberrations are found to have gone uncorrected—a fact apparently not generally appreciated by those using the Munsell system. In consequence, when converting from C.I.E. scores to psychological scores (to or through the Munsell system) the possibility of substantial irregularities must be anticipated whenever variable darkness ("Y" in the C.I.E. system) is involved.

8. Red-purples and yellow-greens do not, of course, fall within this portion of the color circle. In Kenneth L. Kelly and Deane B. Judd, *The ISCC-NBS Method of Designating Colors and A Dictionary of Color Names,* National Bureau of Standards Circular 553 and Standard Sample No. 2106 (Washington, D.C.: The Bureau, 1955; 1965 reissue) some 7,500 color names are listed. With four columns to the page, 44 pages are filled by chromatic colors, of which more than 18 pertain to the red-to-yellow (inclusive) range.

9. The Munsell system places blue-purple (rather than purple) opposite yellow. In terms of existing colorants these two hues appear to be approximately tied for the position of darkest hue. If judged by the available data for the MacAdam limits, the highest intensities that it is theoretically possible to achieve for the twelve basic hues (per Munsell definitions) place purple and blue-purple at the same darkness level (Munsell "value" 4/). All other hues are placed substantially lighter (at 5/ or more). At Munsell "values" 1/, 2/, and 3/, the intensities relative to the highest intensities given for the same hue are significantly greater for purple than for blue-purple.

    If the center of gravity for each of the relevant constant-hue triangles is examined, the center for purple proves to be slightly lower (about Munsell "value" 4.14/ as compared to 4.40/ for blue-purple). In addition, the highest intensity of purple is far greater than that of blue-purple ("chroma" /33 as compared to /20.5).

    For these reasons it would appear more appropriate to think of purple, which for both Munsell and Pope is a basic color, as the darkest of the hues (in opposition to yellow as the lightest).

10. Richard I. Land, in conversations with this writer, commented on the utility of the Pope solid for the artist, designer, and art critic—*based upon its goal of sound generalization and simplicity*—as compared to the use of the Munsell solid by the color scientist and student of vision—*based upon its goal of quantitative scoring in terms of color appearance.*

1. Surprised by the apparent total absence of such representations in color literature, this writer thought that perhaps he was the first to apply the contour method (rather obvious to any cartographer) for defining intensity in terms of hue and darkness (or "value"). It would appear, however, that at least two persons, working independently, somewhat preceded him. In 1967 and 1970 respectively, Louis Rosenblum, a mathematician engaged in color research in association with Morton C. Bradley, and Milton L. Pearson, a color scientist on the staff of the Rochester Institute of Technology's Graphics Arts Research Center, used this graphic method in their color studies. Neither use, however, was ever published. For best graphic readability with such charts, the areas between the contour lines can be shown with gray tones of increasing darkness to suggest increasing intensity.

2. For the scales of the Munsell system, see this Supplement pp. 110-111. Information was supplied in terms of the basic 110 Munsell sampling points on the high intensity surface (for the 10 named Munsell hues, each at the 11 Munsell "value" levels). The highest absolute intensity (or "chroma") ratings per the "nominal notations" for *standard* Munsell glossy samples were used.

   The basic geometry conforms with that recommended by Munsell in the second chapter of *A Color Notation*, though later studies by his followers led to various alternative suggestions. The width of the hue-"value" surface is made approximately π times the height, with the hue circuit split at Munsell red-purple so that Munsell green appears in the center, with blue to the left and red to the right.

   Munsell proposed that the oblique projection (representing absolute intensity) be such that "chroma" /10 equalled the distance from theoretical black to theoretical white. However, usual practice at this time in relation to Munsell color space would employ half that distance. In figure 40 we have made it still less to aid readability and to permit more direct comparison with the display of Pope color space in figure 2.

   If these displays had been based on Munsell data for 40 hues instead of the 10 basic hues assumed, the shape of the resulting surface would of course have been slightly different and more accurate. For example, the contour lines of figure 41 would have had fewer small reversals of direction, the result of interpolation over a greater distance.

   Munsell chips at standard sampling points do not, except by chance, represent the highest intensities achievable with Munsell pigments. The actual gamut surface for such pigments would project somewhat farther by one to two "chroma" units for an average of about one "chroma" unit, and be relatively smooth.

3. Scoring was carried out as follows: Color matches were first made to standard glossy Munsell color chips at all Munsell "values" available between 2/ and 9.25/ inclusive, these being assumed as best representative of typical black and white colorants. Munsell "chroma" was estimated to the nearest even "chroma" score when a chip provided a reasonable match, or by interpolation between chips when necessary. The adequacy of all color matches was then checked by Carpenter (with revisions made as required). From these "chroma" scores, relative intensity was then computed as described in the Supplement, pp. 119-120. Because the hues assumed by Munsell are in part substantially different from those suggested for use with the Pope system, suitable adjustments in spacing were made as required to compensate for the discrepancies. For example, in figure 42 the symbols appear at standard Munsell sampling points. A sharp observer of the color score for the Winslow Homer painting (fig. 4) might wish to question how the intensity indicated at the bottom of the chart just to the right of blue could exist, since intensity at black should be equal to 0%. The intensity shown (of 8%) is the result of the fact that a Munsell "value" greater than zero was assumed for Pope black (namely, Munsell "value" 2/), at which level it is possible to have a "chroma" greater than zero. Black pigments and inks vary in their darkness but appear to average around Munsell "value" 2/, for which reason that figure was assumed as reasonable for use in "mapping" Pope color space. Since the color matching with Munsell chips at standard sampling points is approximate at best, it might not be unreasonable to dispense with the Munsell swatches of a lesser Munsell "value" than 3/. By this means violence to theory could be avoided, at the cost of a slightly more generalized matching process—or, as a possible alternative, a darker black might have been assumed.

4. Such a method for the graphic display of the three basic color variables was almost invented by Munsell. In the second chapter of *A Color Notation*, he speaks of wrapping a cylinder around his color sphere, cutting it at red-purple, and then spreading it out to make a flat chart. Into this he proposed to thrust pins, the length by which each pin projected to be taken as a measure of intensity. But instead of then drawing an oblique line or rod to replace each pin, he stated "we can discard the pin, and record its length by a numeral"—thus sacrificing the benefits of graphic communication to show intensity.

   Munsell used the term "color score" for this type of spread-out color chart. He described it as similar to the musical score by which the "measured relations of sound" are recorded.

5. The SYMAP and SYMVU computer programs were used for the production of these displays, with the gray tone (representing neutral) and the lettering added by hand. The locations for the Munsell hue and "value" combinations, in terms of the Pope color space transformation, were first established, and then the relative intensity scores applicable to each was computed. To assure proper interpolation among and beyond these data locations, additional locations beyond the bottom and top borders were added for Munsell "values" 0/, 1/, and 10/. Similarly, in order to overcome the effect of cutting the color circle at Y, additional locations were added beyond the left and right borders—on the left for Munsell 5Y, 5GY, and 5G, and on the right for Munsell 10YR and 5YR.

   Starting with such data, interpolation among the various locations was then effected by the use of the SYMAP program. The result was a matrix of values at 7,139 locations (59 X 121). Recorded on tape, these were then provided to the SYMVU program which moved an ink pen over paper to produce the final display.

   The SYMAP program was originally developed by the writer; the SYMVU program by Dr. Frank Rens. To anyone interested, the programs are available, together with detailed information on their use, from the Harvard Graduate School of Design's Laboratory for Computer Graphics and Spatial Analysis. (The contour lines of figures 41 and 43 were traced from the SYMAP displays.)

6. Munsell in the second chapter of *A Color Notation* stated: "Flat diagrams . . . are as incomplete as would be a map of Switzerland with the mountains left out, or a harbor chart without indication of the depths of the water."

7. A limitation of the three-dimensional color score is that the darkness of achromatic colors cannot be shown. Actually, true neutrals are only rarely sought in painting, and even more rarely attained. If present, however, that fact can be indicated by providing at the left or right of the diagram, a vertical line reserved exclusively for the representation of neutrals (by a dot). Figures 44 and 45 show the three color variables simultaneously, but this type of display cannot usually be used with success when more than several colors are involved.

8. For the 9 Pope darkness levels the Munsell "value" scores would be as follows: 1 = 9.25/, 2 = 8.34/, 3 = 7.44/, 4 = 6.53/, 5 = 5.62/, 6 = 4.72/, 7 = 3.81/, 8 = 2.91/, 9 = 2.00/.

For those interested in exploring more deeply the problems of darkness scales, the most recent and revealing research (making obsolete much prior work) appears to be that reported by C. C. Semmelroth, "Adjustment of the Munsell-Value and W*-Scales to Uniform Lightness Steps for Various Background Reflectances," *Applied Optics* 10 (January 1971), 14-18. For some insight, even if slight, into the problems of darkness scales in relation to complex fields, see C. J. Bartleson and E. J. Breneman, "Brightness Perception in Complex Fields," *Journal of the Optical Society of America*, 57 (July 1967), 953-957. For higher intensity hues appearing lighter, see C. L. Sanders and G. Wyszecki, "Correlate for Lightness in Terms of CIE Tristimulus Values," *Journal of the Optical Society of America*, 47 (1957), 398-404.

9. See Kenneth L. Kelly and Deane B. Judd, *The ISCC-NBS Method of Designating Col-* ors and *A Dictionary of Color Names*, National Bureau of Standards Circular 553 and Standard Sample No. 2106 (Washington, D. C.: The Bureau, 1955; 1965 reissue). In applying the results of this study several small issues of interpretation were resolved with Mr. Kelly's kind assistance.

10. Munsell was strongly favorable to the use of the metric system, and thought of "chroma" /10 as representing the highest possible absolute intensity for any hue. Today, however, Munsell chips come with ratings as high as /16 or even /16.5 (for "maximum" red-orange which, having no name in the Munsell system, is referred to as hue 10R).

11. The highest intensities for the twelve basic hues pursuant to the combined Munsell and 4-color gamut may vary considerably depending upon the precise hue definitions assumed. For the purpose intended it appeared unwise to employ a narrow definition, and we accordingly interpreted the meaning of each hue designation as embracing (on each side of the ISCC-NBS hue designation) one-quarter of the distance to the next ISCC-NBS hue. In plotting the Munsell high intensities, we employed the highest "chroma" notations recorded in the 1970 listing of Munsell Color Standards, rather than the highest at standard sampling locations. In plotting the 4-color process high intensities, we used the highest intensities achievable with the process inks—based on dot percentages of 0, 5, 10, 20, 30, 40, 50, 60, 70, 80, 90, and 100, as computed by the Rochester Institute of Technology's Graphic Arts Research Center, through the use of what is known as the Neugebauer Equations, and assuming the inks used in the first volume of *ByChrome 4 Color Charts*, that for coated stock. The points representing these were connected with straight lines. Readings of highest "chromas" were then made as described to the nearest one-tenth "chroma" step. For the 12 basic hues they were as follows: Y = /15.7, YO = /16.3, O = /15.8, RO = 16.6, R = /14.3, RP = /15.8, P = /12.6, BP = /13.5, B = /12, BG = /8.6, G = /11.6, YG = /12. Each relative intensity percentage was rounded to the nearest whole percentage figure.

When attempting to illustrate the Pope color solid by color printing, as in color charts 2, 3, and 4, it is obvious that no greater intensities can be shown than can be achieved by the process being used. The only solution is to try to illustrate the concept as well as possible, even if with "high" intensities that are less high than desired.

12. We also checked similarly the acrylic artist's pigments of the "Modular Color" system, as proposed by Nathanial Jacobson and developed by Permanent Pigments, Inc. In one case only, for blue-purple, were they slightly more intense. Some attempt was also made to determine the highest intensities to be procured with commercially available Plexiglas plastics, but by visual inspection these appeared to be of no higher intensity than the combined Munsell and 4-color gamut.

Bibliographies

PUBLISHED WRITINGS OF ARTHUR POPE

Catalogue of Ruskin Exhibition in Memory of Charles Eliot Norton. Cambridge, Mass.: Fogg Art Museum, Harvard University, 1909-1910.

"Tintoretto's Diana," *Art in America,* 9 (October 1916), 353-357.

"A Small Crucifixion by Piero della Francesca," *Art in America,* 10 (August 1917), 217-220.

"Holbein's Portrait of a Musician," *Art in America,* 10 (October 1917), 255-259.

Fine Arts 1A: Outline of Lectures. Cambridge, Mass.: Harvard University, 1919.

Tone Relations in Painting. Cambridge, Mass.: Harvard University Press, 1922. 2d printing, 1926.

Outline of the Theory of Drawing and Painting and Principle of Design. Cambridge, Mass.: Harvard University, Division of Fine Arts, 1924. Reissued 1930, 1936, 1939.

"A Quantitative Theory of Aesthetic Values," *Art Studies* (1925), 133-139.

An Introduction to the Language of Drawing and Painting. Vol. I: *The Painter's Terms.* Vol. II: *The Painter's Modes of Expression.* Cambridge, Mass.: Harvard University Press, 1929-1931. 2d printing, 1939.

George Caleb Bingham, the Missouri Artist, 1811-1879. Exhibition catalogue, January 30-March 7, 1935. New York: Museum of Modern Art, 1935.

Reproductions of Some of the Important Paintings and of Their Details Illustrating the Technique of the Artists. Edited by Arthur Pope and John Davis Hatch, Jr. Boston, Mass.: Isabella Stewart Gardner Museum, 1936.

Art, Artist, and Layman: A Study of the Visual Arts. Cambridge, Mass.: Harvard University Press, 1937.

"Notes on the Problem of Color Harmony and the Geometry of Color Space," *Journal of the Optical Society of America,* 34 (December 1944), 759-765.

Paintings and Drawings of the Pre-Raphaelites and Their Circle. Exhibition catalogue, April 8-June 1, 1946. Cambridge, Mass.: Fogg Art Museum, Harvard University, 1946.

The Language of Drawing and Painting. Cambridge, Mass.: Harvard University Press, 1949. Reprint edition, New York, Russell and Russell, 1967.

Studies in the Art of Painting. Lawrence, Kansas: Museum of Art, University of Kansas, April 1952.

Titian's Rape of Europa: A Study of the Composition and the Mode of Representation in This and Related Paintings. Cambridge, Mass.: Published for the Isabella Stewart Gardner Museum by Harvard University Press, 1960.

Design in Sequence of Time in the So-Called Keion Roll of the Boston Museum. Reprint.

PUBLISHED WRITINGS OF
DENMAN W. ROSS

The Early History of Land-Holding Among the Germans. Boston: Soule and Bugbee, 1883.

Studies in the Early History of Institutions. Cambridge, Mass.: J. Wilson and Son, 1888.

Illustrations of Balance and Rhythm for the Use of Students and Teachers. With Edgar O. Parker and S. Clifford Patchett. Boston: W. B. Clarke Company, 1900.

"Design as a Science," *Proceedings of the American Academy of Arts and Sciences,* 35 (1901), 20.

A Theory of Pure Design. Boston: Houghton Mifflin Company, 1907.

On Drawing and Painting. Boston: Houghton Mifflin Company, 1912.

The Painter's Palette: A Theory of Tone Relations, An Instrument of Expression. Boston: Houghton Mifflin Company, 1919.

Experiments in Drawing and Painting. Exhibition catalogue. New York: Century Association of New York, 1923.

ADDITIONAL READING

Albers, Josef. *Interaction of Color.* Abridged ed. New Haven: Yale University Press, 1971.

Billmeyer, Fred W. Jr., and Saltzman, Max. *Principles of Color Technology.* New York: John Wiley & Sons, 1966.

Birren, Faber. *Principles of Color.* New York: Van Nostrand Reinhold Company, 1969.

Burnham, Robert W., Hanes, Randall M., and Bartleson, C. James. *Color: A Guide to Basic Facts and Concepts.* New York: John Wiley & Sons, 1963.

Evans, Ralph M. *An Introduction to Color.* New York: John Wiley & Sons, 1948.

Hardy, Arthur C., ed. *Handbook of Colorimetry.* Cambridge, Mass: MIT Press, 1936.

Judd, Deane B., and Wyszecki, Günter. *Color in Business, Science, and Industry.* 2d ed. New York: John Wiley & Sons, 1963.

Munsell, Albert H. *A Color Notation.* 12th ed. Baltimore, Md.: Munsell Color Company, Inc., 1967.

——. *A Grammar of Color.* Edited by Faber Birren. New York: Van Nostrand Reinhold Company, 1969.

Murch, Gerald M. *Visual and Auditory Perception.* New York: Bobbs-Merrill Company, 1973.

Optical Society of America, Committee on Colorimetry. *The Science of Color.* Washington, D.C.: Optical Society of America, 1963.

Ostwald, Wilhelm. *The Color Primer.* Edited by Faber Birren. New York: Van Nostrand Reinhold Company, 1969.

Wyszecki, Günter, and Stiles, W. S. *Color Science.* New York: John Wiley & Sons, 1967.

Index

Boldface numbers identify reproductions of works of art. Page references include any notes mentioned thereon; notes are cited directly when discussion of interest might otherwise be overlooked. For some frequently mentioned subjects, only the more significant discussions are cited. There is no entry for Arthur Pope, since the index as a whole may serve as a guide to his basic concepts regarding color in relation to art.

Additive and subtractive processes, 20, 21, 36, 82, 85, 91

Albers, Josef, 29, 37, 45, 46

Anuszkiewicz, Richard: *Inward Eye*, 46, **46**, 53

Attraction, equal visual, 36, 53, 57

Balance in relation to neutral, 16-20

Balance, left and right, 39

Baroque Art, 47, 61, 72, 91

Bazzani, Giuseppe: *Feast in the House of Simon the Pharisee*, 72, **73**, 74, 77

Bonnard, Pierre: *Rue Vue d'en Haut*, 57, **59**

Bukhara School: *Two Figures and a Tree*, **49**, 51, 69

Burchfield, Charles E.: *August Sunlight*, 40, **41**

Byzantine art, 53, 69

Caravaggio, Michelangelo, 61

Cennini, Cennino, 69

Cézanne, Paul: *Auvers, Small Houses*, 51, 72, 74, **75**, 85, 91

Chevreul, Michel, 45

Chroma. *See* Intensity; Munsell

C.I.E., 32, 110, 111, 117, 123 (n. 4), 124 (n. 16), 126 (n. 20), 127 (n. 7)

Colorants, 31, 33, 94, 95, 110, 112, 128 (n. 3). *See also* Pigments in art

Color-blindness, 123 (n. 2)

Color circle, 25, 28, 36, 45, 110, 111, 119, 120; figs. 16, 28, color chart 1. *See also* Hue

Color constancy, 29, 30, 78. *See also* Light, illusion of; Uniformity

Color order systems, 30, 31, 126 (n. 21). *See also* C.I.E.; Munsell; Ostwald

Color scores, 31, 37, 39, 41, 45; figs. 1-4, 40-43

Complementary colors, 36, 41, 111, 123 (n. 4), 124 (n. 13)

Complex fields, 25, 117, 129 (n. 8)

Computer, 37, 45, 124 (n. 16), 127, (n. 3); figs. 1, 3, 4, 40

Constable, John, 72

Constancy. *See* Color constancy; Uniformity

Cool and warm hues, 25, 97, 98, 111

Copley, John Singleton: *Portrait of Colonels Hugo and Schleppergrell*, 83, **84**, 85

Corot, Jean Baptiste Camille, 61, 72

Crowding of darks and lights, 61, 65, 82; fig. 11

Darkness, 24, 25, 96, 110, 115-117; figs. 15, color charts. *See also* Hue-darkness relationships; Value (or darkness) relations in art

Decorative color, 51-57, 69, 72, 88

Degas, Edgar: *At the Races: They're Off!*, 57, **58**

Distance and planes, 53, 57, 58, 69, 72, 78, 82, 88, 91

Equal spacing. *See* Visually equal spacing

Equal visual attraction, 36, 53, 57

First-order descriptions of color variability, 31, 33, 37, 106-108, 110, 111

Flemish art, 58

Flicker color, 123 (n. 1)

Fluorescence, 112, 123 (n. 6)

Fragonard, Jean Honoré: *Le Premier Pas de l'Enfance*, **74**, 74

Gaugin, Paul, 51, 69

Gérard, Marguerite: *Le Premier Pas de l'Enfance*, **74**, 74

Giotto, 69

Gombrich, E. H., 61

Gothic art, 69

Gradation. *See* Sequence

Gray. *See* Neutral

Guston, Philip: *Summer, 1954*, 37, **38**, 39, 41, 45, 51, 57, **114**, 115; figs. 1, 7, 42, 43

Hals, Frans: *Portrait of a Preacher*, **83**, 83, 85

Hartley, Marsden: *Landscape*, 53, **54**

Hassam, Childe: *Headlands,* 78, 80, 82

Homer, Winslow: *Canoe in the Rapids,* 41, **43**, 45, 46, 57, 115, 128 (n. 3); figs. 4, 6; *Homosassa Jungle in Florida,* **76**, 77; *The Trapper, Adirondacks,* **77**, 78

Hopper, Edward: *Libby House, Portland, Maine,* 40, 41; *Highland Light,* 61, **62**

Hue, 25, 28, 96, 97, 110, 111, 117, 118; fig. 16, color charts

Hue-darkness relationships, 33, 97, 108, 110, 111, 112, 117; color charts

Hue relations in art, 46

Impressionism, 35, 36, 58, 61, 82, 85

Indian art, 68, 69

Indiana, Robert: *Art (Red, Blue, and Green Art),* **50**, 51

Intensity, 28, 97, 111, 112, 118-120; fig. 17. *See also* Relative intensity

Intensity relations in art, 65, 68, 82; fig. 12

Interaction of colors, 16, 24, 29, 37, 45, 46

Inter-Society Color Council, ISCC-NBS hues, 118

Isolated color, 16, 17, 41

Japanese art, 68

Klee, Paul, 69

Light. *See* Viewing light; Color constancy

Light, illusion of, 58, 61, 69, 77, 78, 82. *See also* Color constancy

Light waves, 13-21, 78, 95

Lightness. *See* Darkness

Limitation of color range, 37-51

Linear mode, 68, 69

Lorenzetti, Ambrogio: *Crucifixion,* 69, **71**

Louis, Morris: *Color Barrier,* 40, 41

Master of the Fogg Pietà: *Mourning Over the Body of Christ,* 69, **70**, 72, 85; fig. 13

Matisse, Henri: Plates from *Jazz,* 51, **52**, 53, 57

Modeling, 47, 58, 69, 72, 77, 83, 91

Models of color space, 30, 113; cover

Monet, Claude: *Fish,* **60**, 61, 69, 77; fig. 10; *Route de la Ferme St. Simeon, Honfleur,* 61, **63**; *La Cabane du Douanier,* 69, **81**, 82

Moore, Charles Herbert, 35

Mosaics, 53

Munsell, Albert H., and system: Munsell solid, 32, 33, 36, 110-112, 113, 114, 124 (n. 16); three-variable displays, 128 (n. 4), 129 (n. 6), figs. 40, 41; metric system, 129 (n. 10); "chroma" vs. relative intensity, 28, 118, 119; highest "chromas" as 100% intensity, 120; scores used, 112, 114, 118, 127 (ns. 3, 6, 7) 128 (ns. 3, 5); mentioned, 94, 117, 120, 124 (n. 10), 125 (n. 20), 127 (n. 4), 129 (n. 8)

National Bureau of Standards, 117, 118, 120

Neutral, 13-17, 24, 95, 96, 98, 112, 115, 129 (n. 7); color chart 1

Optical Society of America, 126 (n. 20), 127 (n. 7)

Order in art, 36, 39, 41. *See also* First-order descriptions of color variability

Ostwald, Wilhelm, 32, 120, 124 (n. 16)

Oudry, Jean Baptiste: *Woodcock and Quail,* 85, **87**

Palette, 36, 68, 83, 85. *See also* Pigments in art

Persian School, Qazuin: *Youth with Bow and Arrows,* **49**, 69

Phillips, Ammi: *Portrait of Harriet Leavens,* **50**, 51

Picasso, Pablo: *Abstraction III* and *IV,* 55, 57

Pictorial mode, 72, 74, 77, 88

Pigments in art, 36, 61, 82, 85, 88. *See also* Palette; Colorants

Pissarro, Camille, 82

Planes. *See* Distance and planes

Pointillism, 20; *also see* 82, 85, 91

Portraits, 83, 85

Post-impressionism, 85

Prendergast, Maurice Brazil: *Beach, New England,* **56**, 57

Primary colors, 25, 117

Printing, 20, 31, 110, 120

Proportional relations, 58, 61, 65; figs. 11, 12

Rajput School: *Krishna and Attendants in Chariot,* **48**, 68

Regular change. *See* Sequence

Relative intensity, 28, 94, 107, 111, 118-120, 123 (n. 7). *See also* Intensity

Renaissance, 69

Renoir, Pierre Auguste: *At the Milliner's,* 85, **86**; *Spring Bouquet,* 88, **89**

Representational color, 41, 51, 57, 58, 61, 65, 68

Rochester Institute of Technology, 117, 124 (n. 9), 128 (n. 1)

Rococo art, 72, 91

Roman art, 72

Ross, Denman W., 31, 32, 35, 36, 94, 96, 117

Rubens, Peter Paul: *Quos Ego,* 46, **47**, 48, 51, 57, 72, 74, 77, 85; fig. 8

Ruisdael, Jacob van: *A Road Lined with Trees,* **64**, 65, 72

Runge, Philip Otto, 32

Sampling locations, 102, 106, 110, 112, 125 (n. 20), 128 (ns. 2, 3); figs. 30-32, color charts

Scales, 96. *See* Darkness, Hue, Intensity; *also* C.I.E., Munsell, Visually equal spacing

Sculptural mode, 69, 72, 77

Second-order descriptions of color variability, 33, 106-110; fig. 33

Sequence, 39, 41, 46, 53, 74

Sheeler, Charles: *Upper Deck,* 78, **79**

Signac, Paul: *La Rochelle,* 65, 68, **68**

Simultaneous and successive contrast, 29, 45, 53

Simultaneous display of color variables, 31, 113-115; figs. 1-4, 34-45

Simultaneous functions of color in art, 82-91

Sisley, Alfred: *Le Pont de Conflans à Moret,* 65, **66**

Solids. *See* Color order systems

Space, illusion of, 57, 58. *See also* Distance and planes

Spreading effect, 46, 53

Stained glass, 53, 123 (n. 7)

Subtractive and additive processes, 20, 21, 36, 82, 85, 91

Surface color, 13, 21, 112, 120, 123 (n. 5)

Theory in art, 35, 36, 68; *also see* Preface

Tiepolo, Giovanni Domenico: *Apotheosis of Aeneas,* 72, 74, 88, **90**, 91; fig. 14

Titian (Tiziano Vecelli), 72

Toulouse-Lautrec, Henri de: *Trapeze Artist at the Medrano Circus,* **56**, 57; fig. 9

Translucence, 20, 21, 53, 85, 123 (n. 7)

Turner, J. M. W.: *Simplon Pass,* 41, **42**, 45, 46, 65, 72, 82, 115; figs. 3, 5; *Ehrenbreitstein,* 65, **67**, 68, 72

Two-variable diagrams, 30, 45, 97, 98, 101, 102, 115; figs. 5-10, 12-14, 18-20, 23-24

Uniformity, 39, 41, 46, 53; of attraction, 36, 53, 57, 69

Value (or darkness) relations in art, 47, 51, 61. *See also* Darkness

Van Eyck, Jan, 58

Venetian art, 72

Vermeer, Jan, 58, 61

Viewing light, 16, 20, 21

Visual mode, 58, 77, 78, 82, 88

Visually equal spacing, 24, 25, 33, 37, 94, 96, 115, 117, 127 (n. 3)

Vuillard, Edouard, *L'Atre,* 57, **58**

Warm and cool hues, 25, 97, 98, 111

Wavelengths, 13-21, 78, 95

James M. Carpenter is Professor of Art and Chairman of the Art Department at Colby College, Waterville, Maine. He received his A.B. and Ph.D. from Harvard, and taught at Harvard under Arthur Pope. During the years that Pope was Director of the Fogg Art Museum Mr. Carpenter carried on the courses in the theory of art that Pope had established. Since 1950 he has been involved with the development of the Art Department and the Art Museum at Colby College. His teaching has moved primarily into the area of art history but is strongly based in a theoretical approach to the study of works of art.

Mr. Carpenter has written a portion of the book *Maine and Its Role in American Art* and numerous exhibition catalogues. He has organized *Art in the Making,* an exhibition of unfinished paintings, as well as several exhibitions on Maine art. He is a member of the Board of Governors of the Skowhegan School of Painting and Sculpture, a trustee of the Haystack Mountain School of Crafts, and has served for six years as a member of the Maine State Commission on the Arts and Humanities.

Howard T. Fisher is a member of the faculty of the Harvard Graduate School of Design. Formerly Professor of City Planning, he currently serves as Research Professor of Cartography. Born in 1903, he studied art history at Harvard College, and was graduated in 1926. He devoted more than twenty-five years to the professional practice of architecture and city planning, and to research on building materials and construction methods. In 1957 Mr. Fisher joined the faculty of the Technological Institute at Northwestern University, where he designed the SYMAP program for computer mapping, a widely used system for the machine display of spatially variable information. Invited to Harvard in 1964, he established and became the first director of its Laboratory for Computer Graphics and Spatial Analysis.

As a Harvard student in the 1920s, Mr. Fisher first became acquainted with Arthur Pope. In 1970 his interest in the use of color as a quantitative analogue in mapping led him to undertake a serious investigation of Pope's work. His contribution to this publication is the result of his firm belief in the special virtues of Pope's concepts from the viewpoint of the creative artist and designer.